The Really REALLY Bad News Bible

Pugnacious Loyola

aka Paul Schmidt

CONTENTS

The Really REALLY Bad News Bible

ACKNOWLEDGMENTS

Special thanks to Karma Ruder, Myrna Schlegel, and Diane Nelson for their tremendous support and contribution to this book. Over the past fifteen years Karma has not only given me wonderful, sometimes hard feedback, but has also done all of the prep work required to bring this project to fruition. She also handled a huge portion of the editing! Myrna Schlegel did the final round of editing, finding more errors than I thought possible, and she offered an insightful set of questions and comments that resulted in a much better book. Diane also provided excellent feedback and assisted with the editing. Like Karma, she helped light a fire under me when it came to my more succinctly finishing the book's Conclusion.

Special thanks also to Steve Bhaerman aka Swami Beyondananda (www.wakeuplaughing.com) and Mark Monlux (www.markmonlux.com). Steve wrote the Preface and the chapter headers, and in bringing the Swami's uproarious presence into my life, has gifted me with the "pun-damentalist" jousting partner I always wanted. Gifted illustrator Mark Monlux designed the book's cover, giving life to Pugnacious Loyola.

Finally, it is important to acknowledge American luminary Thomas Paine and the late freethinker, C. Dennis McKinsey. The respective writings of these two intellectual giants, *The Age of Reason* and *The Encyclopedia of Biblical Errancy* have served as the foundation of my research on the Bible.

PREFACE

The "Really REALLY Bad News Bible" Is Really Good News…From Buying Bull to Bye-Bye Bull

by Steve Bhaerman aka Swami Beyondananda

"There are so many versions of the story, it's hard to tell crucifixion from crucifact."

-- Swami Beyondananda

Paul Schmidt has been in dogged pursuit of truth since I've known him, and in his magnum opus (until now, anyway), he takes on "the greatest story ever told", as he hoists the Bible on its own petard of contradictions and puzzling statements.

While I would never deign to tread on what 2.3 billion Christians, 1.8 billion Muslims and 14 million Jews consider sacred turf, Paul has no such compunctions. He combed that fine couth tome with a fine-toothed comb, and in his mission to discern crucifixion from crucifact (a provable event historians agree happened, with artifacts, etc.) he has come up with a readable and provocative romp through the Book responsible for more death and destruction than all the plagues combined.

This in and of itself should justify this irreverently uplifting "work of heart".

The Really REALLY Bad News Bible is a mixture of dark (and light) humor, sprinkled with a mind-boggling array of biblical contradictions that should drive any true believer crazy. Or, as Paul suggests, maybe craziness is a pre-existing condition.

While Christianity and the Church have produced St. Francis and Mother Teresa, they have also produced the Crusades, the Inquisition, and the subjugation, exploitation and extinction of the Native populations of the New World. Did you know ... that the Inter Caetera papal bull (pun not intended, but duly noted) issued by Pope Alexander VI May 4, 1493 called for non-Christian nations to be reduced and subjugated ("barbare nationes deprimantur")?

Not only did this innocuous-sounding "doctrine of discovery" justify and fuel the destruction of the Native cultures in the Americas and the pillaging of its resources, it has also been used by our U.S. Supreme Court to abrogate treaties with the Native American peoples!

Put another way, Columbus "discovered" America like Willie Sutton* "discovered" banks.

Still, the Bible and religion seek to connect us with the Divine, eternal and ineffable. Let's remember the original meaning of religion comes from the Latin, religare, to bind. At its best, religious practice connects us to the Great Spirit, our inner soul, the web of life, and other humans.

At worst ... well as some great pundit once said, spirituality is our connection to the Divine. Religion is crowd-control.

As a Sufi teacher observed, every great prophet and spiritual visionary heard what they perceived as an awesome symphony ... but when codified into religious doctrine, the symphony becomes a plaintive "kazoo bleat."

And the bleat goes on.

Which is why this book is such a helpful remedy for those who've been abused -- or even bemused -- by organized religion. And while some humans might find the style or some of the content

4

offensive, I have complete trust that the Creator -- not being an actual "person" after all -- won't take it Personally.

In fact, it might be that the Jesus who embraced the Beatitudes and kicked the money changers out of the temple would recognize the good news" in this Bad News Bible, that the Old Testament Christians who see "God-fearing" as more important than "Life-loving" would likely miss.

So enjoy the guilty pleasure of reading this book. Even if you're a devout believer, you will find something to chuckle about -- and guaranteed, you'll learn something you didn't know before. Paul did his homework!

Steve Bhaerman
*Willie Sutton was a famous bank robber.

INTRODUCTION

There's a bumper sticker which is quite popular in the United States that reads: CHRIST IS THE ANSWER. Not to be a wiseass here, but I can't help but wonder: If Christ is the answer, then what is the question? The response will likely vary for Christians of the over thirty thousand plus denominational persuasions worldwide. For those located somewhere in the evangelical/fundamentalist zone of the spectrum, the answer will be guided by hope of personal salvation as dictated by "God-given truths," and there will always be an extreme sense of urgency about this. I mean, who wants to burn in hell, right?

In my own personal history, I was definitely no stranger to the pursuit of this kind of personal salvation, a pursuit consuming a period of several decades. I was raised Catholic and grew up devoutly, almost becoming a Trappist monk, even as I did finally avoid getting trapped. After a brief U-Turn into atheism during my college years, (a move almost any self-respecting student needs to explore), I had two unexpected paranormal experiences which put me firmly back on the path of religious inquiry -- you know, the one in which curiosity delights in killing the cat. From that point on, and almost to the age of 40, I moved from one religious experience to the next, and sometimes back again, seeking the "One Truth" that would allegedly lead to personal salvation. Each time I believed, even up to several years per stint, that I had found it. And the gyrations were wild: taking me from one "authoritative" guru to the next, and from religions as varied as Pentecostal Christianity to fundamentalist Hinduism. Giving up control of my life to leaders who claimed to understand the nature of reality and had scriptures to "prove" it became second nature to me, even as this repeated descent into foolishness made me miserable each time.

Those days are over, and thank heavens! I no longer believe in gurus and their so called "sacred scriptures." This does not mean I disbelieve in God and an afterlife. In fact, I'd venture to say I'm

95% sure these exist, even though I suppose the stubborn 5% does make me something of an agnostic, if a grudging one. And, based on my own paranormal and Out of Body Experiences (OBEs), as well as the immense volume of anecdotal evidence out there regarding Near Death Experiences (NDEs), I'm pretty sure we do continue after death, even though I know it cannot be proven. What I am sure of though, and 100% sure, is that if any of us is going to have a guru, best to find that guru inside ourselves.

In any case, as much as I hope that I continue beyond the grave (and you too!), I no longer aspire to personal salvation in an afterlife as the focus of my quest. If I'm saved, great. But as D.H. Lawrence said, "Life is to be spent, not saved." Best to invest in helping make the world a better place and to relegate the rest to mystery.

Easier said than done, letting go of the need for assurances transcending time and space? Maybe, but why not give it a try? It is thrilling to note that the marketing of this type of personal salvation is a harder and harder sell these days, and not least because the quest for archaic God archetypes is increasingly being displaced and replaced by keener and keener interest in the evolution of what we know through science, on the one hand, and friendlier post-damnation spirituality, on the other. Selling the personal salvation investment perspective, even using the carrot-stick approach involving sweet words about eternal paradise, but also threats of eternal hell, doesn't work quite as well as it used to, people no longer being so easily manipulated.

Let's face it: just because a religion is old doesn't mean it is viable. Difficult as it may be for some to hear, the various questionable elements of Christianity and other religions that have been around long enough to acquire the pungent smell of dogma, are being increasingly exposed under the hot, bright lights of energetic investigation. In a word, we can more and more clearly see that, religious fundamentalist denial notwithstanding, there's something not quite right with alleged holy scriptures like the Bible. Some of the stories contained therein simply don't make much sense, not from a perspective of either logic or ethics, nor as a source of the inspiration required to bring forth a new world paradigm in which tolerance, kindness, and love prevail.

Even those persons generally prone to belief in a Higher Power who may be authentically searching for some version of the sacred, now routinely conclude that their quest doesn't have to restrict itself to any particular religious prescription or ideology including that which claims that Jesus (and Jesus alone) saves. Nevertheless, becoming too Pollyannaish regarding the big picture is likely ill-advised. Why? Well, for starters, a fairly recent Gallup Poll showed that 24% of Americans apparently believe that the Bible should be read as the literal Word of God. Another 47% still think that the Bible is the inspired Word of God.

The point here is, if you add up the power held by these two groups of people, it's not hard to see that what is popularly believed about the content of the Bible, whether true or not, dramatically informs not only our culture, but likely the consciousness of numerous future generations as well. The hypnotic power of the Bible is especially disturbing when those who carry significant political power use their fundamentalist interpretation of scripture as a gyroscopic guide for less-than "Christian" policy. This brings to mind Swami Beyondananda's observation regarding the rigidly-religious: "The problem with fundamentalists is, they've put the mental before the fun." As Swami further comments, these folks are really to be considered the "no fun-damentalists," those who likely "get mad at their Higher Self" because "it's always getting high without them."

This little book has been written for those who are ready to reconsider in a deeper way just what it is that the Bible actually is offering us and what it fails to offer us. It has been written for those who are ready to help redirect human consciousness away from anachronistic religious influence and salvation marketing, and to perhaps save the world in the process. This may well mean differentiating with greater skill between the free thinker-friendly practice of contemplating ideas about what makes a good life for ourselves and our planetary neighbors, and the unthinking acceptance of what has become a foundational religious document written thousands of years ago and reflecting a less evolved society. To wade into this discussion, one must recognize that, misplaced faith aside, reading the Bible in a responsible way definitely requires not only critical thinking, but also hip boots and a good sense of humor, hopefully one which is not entirely alien to the irreverent.

Now don't get me wrong: not for a minute am I suggesting that the Christian Bible is entirely devoid of nuggets of truth or all ethical value. And yet, while the Bible does have its moments, as for example when Jesus says to forgive seventy times seven (Matthew 18:22), these are sporadic. Taken as a whole, the Bible simply doesn't pass the smell test, not if you are looking for a scripture founded on love and wisdom.

The fact that the Bible has endured through the ages is less a testimony to its greatness as a scripture than to the willingness of many Christian readers to not really invest in seeing what is actually in front of them. Of course, endeavoring to read this strange scripture from alpha to omega, or, more specifically, from Genesis to Revelation is an onerous, even emotionally herniating task. Far more Christians than not have simply chosen to take professional clergy's word for what the biblical authors intended. And let's face it, if the clergy is expert at anything besides mass hypnosis, it is the art of cherry picking verses for the purpose of radical scriptural sanitation.

This little book is a gratefully shorter read than the Bible, and will demonstrate how crazy-sounding this scripture actually is. Frankly, the Bible is a bizarre conglomerate of false prophecies, insufferable violence, pathologically-infected morality, environmental terrorism, and even falsely recorded Hebrew history. For example, modern archeology has now conclusively proven that the walls of Jericho had already crumbled long before the Israelite army even arrived. The stories of the wall of Jericho miraculously tumbling down are fraudulent indeed! And even if that hadn't been the case, teaching Sunday School children to celebrate the mass murder of an entire city population is as unethical as it is shockingly disgraceful.

I need to state something here unequivocally: my book is in no way intended as an attack on 'God' or the sacred, only on that idea of 'God' and his alleged 'Only Begotten Son' as represented in the Bible. Frankly I am not certain these two entities even exist non-fictionally. In Jesus Christ's case, it would seem like what we are looking at is a mix of fiction and non-fiction, myth and reality, much like Davy Crockett, although obviously, far more compelling and powerful.

My intention is to lampoon the fruits of the Bible writers who have presented us with a weird smorgasbord of claims about the nature of reality and God, as if their bizarre offerings are somehow synonymous with eternal Truth. Sorting out what the Bible has to say about the Israelites and their relationship to Yahweh, and especially what it has to say about Yahweh/God and/or Jesus Christ, is important. If we know anything, it's that people have always been highly proficient in the dark art of bold, outrageous fabrication, even while posing as truth sayers. For any number of reasons, including the cunning will-to-power that tops that list, dishonest people seeking control, and authority over others have historically made up all sorts of crazy-sounding things, many of which have stuck.

If the saying that we are known by our fruits is true, the same must be conceded regarding books, especially scriptural books claiming to be holy and wholly beyond reproach. Otherwise, what we end up with is the fruit of the spirit made rotten, not only with falsehood, but also the will to take itself too seriously. It was of course British philosopher A. N. Whitehead who said that the most singular thing about the Bible is its lack of a sense of humor, and I couldn't agree more!

My criticism of the Bible and its priest craft notwithstanding, I am well aware that there are many wonderful Christians in the world today, folks who, per Jesus Christ's alleged advice, would not only walk the extra mile with you in a crisis, but literally give you the shirts and blouses off their backs. Many of these go on missions to help those in dire need; many others generously give tithes and offerings to their church of choice and many other really wonderful social causes. And make no mistake: whether you want to talk in terms of movement of the Holy Spirit or, let's say, misidentified paranormal activity in church settings, something peculiar seems to be going on in a number of churches, especially of the Pentecostal ilk. In any case, many Christians are simply terrific and, in terms of historical perspective, have suffered, been tortured and even died for their faith.

On the other hand, some Christians, brainwashed by corrupt Christian institutions, have killed and tortured countless souls throughout the ages, especially in the Middle Ages. Two well-known horrible examples, out of potential thousands, are the mass murder of women and girls via the Catholic Inquisition, and the so-called holy Crusades. In the case of the Inquisition, the ideologues in charge sadistically managed to transport Revelation's proverbial "Lake of Fire" from the realm of horrible scriptural imagination into the physical realm. Consequently, hundreds of thousands of women and girls, including those with a mere passion for medicinal herbs and healing, were burnt alive in Europe as witches, or in fewer cases, strangled to death. With regard to the hideous Crusades, the most psychopathic among the Crusaders tortured and massacred victims of all ages, sometimes even roasting children alive on spits. They of course did so confidently in the name of Jesus Christ.

As long as the Bible and other scriptures like it sustain an overt or even covert politico-military bent, the world will remain in very deep danger, risking the nightmare inherent in the anonymous quote: "History keeps repeating itself because no one is listening." The notion that the embers of the hell-on-earth which the fathers of the Inquisition, the Crusaders, and other offenders incited and engineered are not still glowing is a dangerous, absurd falsehood. They absolutely are, and until we clean up our act as human beings, simultaneously dispensing with psychopathy and theocracy in favor of a free and freely-tolerant global paradigm, the threat of unchecked hell-on-earth will remain alive and well here on crazy planet earth.

For the purposes of this book, I'm interested in presenting at least enough Bible passages across an array of topics to have this scripture demonstrate to you by its own words that, far from being the inspired Word of God, it is written by men, apparently very flawed men, who can only offer us a cacophony of woefully ignorant, often mean-spirited nonsense spread out among sixty-six books. The idea that well-meaning people seeking some semblance of the sacred need to swallow the Bible wholesale would be a joke, if only the massive biblical brainwashing were not so prevalent and effective. And-speaking of the sacred, it's important to understand that the presumptuous notion that the sacred somehow belongs only to those who believe in God and/or an afterlife is as arrogant as it ridiculous. Sacredness is the domain or potential domain of all authentic persons, whatever their beliefs.

The material presented in the main body of this book generally tends to err, if err it does, on the side of the unabashedly irreverent, the idea being to help in some small way to raise Christianity and humanity from the grave or even the semi-serious. As I've suggested, what I've taken aim at is not the alleged Jesus Christ or God the Father, given that it is unclear to me whether these two even exist, at least in the way the Bible wants us to know them. The target here is the body of biblical writings (the alleged Word of God) that claim to represent these figures accurately and as actual, factual Beings worthy of our faith and worship. Whoever or whatever the biblical Jesus Christ and His dad may or may not be, they are not Beings worthy of being revered given the behaviors portrayed in the Bible.

In saying this I'd be naive not to recognize that some of you are already taking umbrage with me, thinking that whatever problems the Bible may have, it is the Word of God and therefore how dare I take on its two most reverenced heroes, Yahweh and Jesus Christ? I invite you to keep reading, and in so doing, to examine what irreverence regarding your God actually feels like, and why that is. Please remember, my irreverence is not directed at God or Jesus Christ – but rather at these characters as portrayed. The Bible is a book, for Christ's sake! And one that has a lot of nonsense, as we shall explore. But consider this, if you would: when religion tries to box in the sacred, making it fit within the lines of "scripture", the sacred has no choice but to escape. That which is truly sacred cannot be controlled and manipulated. It lives within each of us as something fiercely spontaneous and independent, and simply cannot be confined. Dogma, even that which calls itself the Word of God, is nothing more than a counterfeit of the sacred.

While some Christians still look to a planetary future featuring Armageddon and the so-called Rapture, more and more of us conversely seek a comedy ending to the Armageddon Script and a rapturous parting of the ways with anachronistic religion. A new world beckons to us, one in which the darkly hypnotic influence of bad biblical ideas simply dies, being gratefully laughed to death, the spell being broken for all time. This will take no doubt take some work, but even more, it will take play including wordplay, the pen and keyboard hopefully being mightier than the sword or even ICBMs. After fifteen years of wrestling with the angels of biblical ignorance, stupidity and solemnity, this little book is my offering to you. Blessed are the mirthful, for you shall obtain mirth.

Chapter One: MEET JESUS CHRIST'S DADDY

"Who doesn't want to have a warm, fuzzy dogma to snuggle up with on a dark night of the soul?"
-- Swami Beyondananda

Surprising as it may be to true believers, not everyone in the early Church happened to agree with the Epistle of James' assertion that the deity depicted in scripture was anyone, anything resembling "the perfect gift-giving Father of Lights in whom there is no variance" (James 1:17). For the Gnostics who spoke the truth, as they esoterically understood it, during the first and second centuries before having their proverbial vocal chords cut by the orthodox, the God of the Old Testament was problematic in the extreme. For some Gnostics, Yahweh was a darkly egotistic and maniacal demiurge from the lower astral plane, while for others, He was actually Satan. Suffice it to say, neither of these groups were especially inclined to worship Him, considering such worship a fool's errand and a betrayal of the Light.

If we try and take the Bible and its projected deity as a whole, the argument can convincingly be made that James 1:17 appears to be something akin to false advertising. It is part of the New Testament marketing material to present God as warm and fuzzy, a supreme source of enduring love. Unfortunately, the Old Testament God whom Jesus Christ enthusiastically endorses, right along with this God's law and prophets (Matthew 5:17), is shockingly dark, and not just on occasion, being the self-admitted author of evil (Isaiah 45:7). Far from operating as a Presence beyond all shadow or even any Jungian shadow of a doubt, Yahweh disturbingly overshadows humanity and the world.

Take for example the intended premeditated sacrifice of Isaac by his father Abraham, a guy who was big on following the voices he heard in his head. It is but one of legion examples given straight faced in the Bible of deadly, violent intent mistaken for holiness, and in most cases, it's macabre fulfillment. Being an equal opportunity destroyer, the biblical God isn't even remotely above mass murder of people representing all ages including infants and toddlers (Ezekiel 9:5,6). Neither is Yahweh remotely adverse to commanding the rape, torture, disfigurement, and enslavement of His enemies. You know this, or would know this, if you've read the Bible.

Given the savagery of the biblical God, as portrayed, is it any wonder the English poet, painter, print maker and esoteric William Blake referred to the Judeo-Christian God, not as "Heavenly Father", but as Nobodaddy (Nobody's daddy)? As the brilliant Robert Anton Wilson aptly points out, the biblical God is vain beyond measure and has the emotions of a five-year-old, being, as He is, prone to foul moods, petty jealousies, and murderous temper tantrums.

Gnostic spin doctors may have done their awkward best to divorce Jesus Christ from Yahweh. But the process fails miserably. Remember, Jesus Christ came, not to abolish the Old Testament God's, law and prophets, but to fulfill them. This Father-Son team is tight! Buyer, beware.

By His own admission, humans were created for His own glory (Isaiah 43:7). No one dared speak up and say, "It's all about you, Lord, isn't it?"

Oddly enough, the Bible wants you to know that love is not jealous (1 Corinthians 13:4), even if the biblical God is (Deuteronomy 4:24). The confusing plot thickens when we learn that the biblical God is supposedly love (1 John 4:8).

If you happened to be a boy and also the oldest son in the family in ancient Israel, you were likely toast inasmuch as Yahweh demanded that your parents sacrifice you to Him (Exodus 22:29). So much for your brother bitching about his middle child complex!

Yahweh repeats, as He does so often, that He is the Lord and then adds that He doesn't change (Malachi 3:6). But the truth is, wearing the same clothes day in and day out is not particularly hygienic, even for God.

The time will apparently come when the Lord will begin healing the wounds He inflicted on His people and He'll do this by making the moon as bright as the sun, and the sun itself 7x's brighter (Isaiah 30:26). Be that as it may, your circadian rhythm will be altered forever and your ability to sleep, utterly destroyed.

Demonstrating a profound commitment to the Sixth Commandment which He Himself created (Thou shalt not kill), Yahweh commands the obedient thusly: "Kill them all--old and young, girls and women and little children" (Ezekiel 9:6).

Never mind that lying lips are an abomination unto the Lord God Yahweh (Proverbs 12:22). By His own admission, He puts a lying spirit into the mouths of certain prophets (1 Kings 22:23), thus proving that politicians, lawyers, and cheating spouses don't have an exclusive on forked-tongue communication.

Ezekiel 21:37 is about burning fat, but not in the preferred pounds-shedding sense. In this passage, Yahweh warns the Ammonites that He shall make them fuel for the fire.

We are told in Numbers 16:49 that the biblical God slaughtered with a plague 14,700 of His chosen people simply because they murmured about their crappy leaders, Moses and Aaron. This mass murder from on high no doubt helped the survivors work on murmuring less, much less.

The biblical God declares that He will send hornets to destroy any surviving soldiers (Deuteronomy 7:30) in one particular battle. Now, due to meticulous NBA record keeping, we can safely surmise this wasn't the lowly Charlotte Hornets.

Make sure your children don't disobey or defy the biblical God or He may turn you into a cannibal, causing you to eat your kids' flesh (Deuteronomy 28:53). To add insult to profound injury, you might consequently end up having to raise your grandchildren.

Apparently pissed off, the biblical God threatens to make Israelites eat meat till it comes out of their noses (Numbers 11:18-20). Although this threat likely converted a number of God's Chosen to vegetarianism, those who ended up victims quickly discovered the appalling uselessness of nasal decongestants.

The biblical God says to Moses: "And I will take away my hand and you will see my back parts, but my face shall not be seen." (Exodus 33:23). Call it what you like, but it sure sounds like Yahweh mooned the unsuspecting Moses.

Forget about trying to locate handicapped parking spaces in the Bible zone. If you had any kind of disability, you weren't even allowed into the sanctuary, your very presence being a profanity in the sight of the biblical God (Leviticus 21:17-21).

Yahweh tells the Israelites to vex the Midianites and to smite them (Numbers 25:17). Given the opportunity to choose between the two, the Midianites would no doubt have enthusiastically preferred to be vexed.

Perhaps suffering a hangover, Yahweh complains to His prodigal son Satan that he (Satan) has enticed Him into ruining his faithful servant Job (Job 2:3). Never mind the contradictory biblical claim that God cannot be tempted with evil (James 1:13).

As the consequence of a Vegas-style wager between Yahweh and His son Satan, Job is made to suffer innumerable horrors, the most egregious being the murder of his children. The story has a happy ending, however, inasmuch as Job is ultimately blessed with a reversal of fortune including the divine kindness of having all the dead kids replaced with brand new ones (Job 42:1-17).

The biblical God smites His humble servant Job with boils from the top of his head to the bottom of his feet (Job 2:7). According to Proverbs 12:21, this kind of health misfortune or any kind of misfortune only befalls the wicked, a claim that would no doubt have millions of Christians scratching their heads, if only they had actually read the Bible.

Malachi 2:3 raises many a pair of eyebrows in stating: "Not only will God corrupt your kids, he'll spread dung all over your faces." This indubitably gives a whole new meaning to the quaint phrase, "getting shit faced."

In Deuteronomy 28:22 the biblical God lists seven means by which He will kill people. The seventh, mildew, would no doubt have been of particular concern to those living in the Pacific Northwest or especially central Florida.

Perhaps concerned with lower back pain issues, King David assembles a host of 30,000 to move the Ark of the Covenant. A soldier named Uzzah errs in trying to steady the Ark when a team of oxen make it tip and he is promptly rewarded from on high by being struck dead.

Curiosity is entirely capable of killing much more than the cat. For example, 50,070 men of Beth Shemesh are mass murdered by the biblical God on account of a few of them looking inside the erotica- friendly Ark of the Covenant (1 Samuel 6:19).

Whoever strikes one of his or her parents is to be put to death (Exodus 21:15). Yo, dip shit, there goes your allowance!

If a woman is proven (apparently by gynecological-astute priests) not to be a virgin on her wedding night, she is to be stoned to death on the doorstep of her father's house by the entire town (Deuteronomy 20:20-21). Whether or not the town was invited inside for refreshments after the event goes unmentioned.

Being a God who values choice, Yahweh offers King David three options for mass murdering his own people. Perhaps after a game of "Rock, Paper, Scissors", David chooses pestilence, and the final body count ends up topping 70,000 (First Chronicles 21:12-14).

In Leviticus 22:9, Yahweh states that we are to obey His rules or else He will kill us. Clear enough for you?

Except that the Holy Bible calls for the execution of any child who cusses at or disobeys his mom or dad (see Leviticus 20:9, Deuteronomy 20:18-21, Exodus 21:17), it is decidedly pro-child, pro-family, pro-life. And the Church said "Amen"?

Do you have any doubts that need to be dispelled about Yahweh not being the Higher Power celebrated at AA meetings? In Jeremiah 25:27 the biblical God tells a certain group of unfortunates: "Drink, get drunk and vomit, and rise no more because the sword I will send among you."

The biblical God wants you to hack the sons and daughters of His enemies (Ezekiel 23:36-47). What's unclear here is whether these people have sufficient firewall and anti-virus protection to withstand these divinely-ordained cyberattacks.

Biblical law once required the death penalty for those who work on the Sabbath (Exodus 31:14-15). On a more positive note, there's no mention of the condemned having been subject to any kind of monetary fine.

Never mind the threat of death for exerting yourself on the Sabbath (Exodus 31:14). If your ass falls into a pit on this holy day, you'll likely want to pull it out (Luke 14:5) since, otherwise, your head and limbs and much of your torso will remain down there, too.

Psalm 136:26 calls on us to give thanks to the God of heaven, saying that His steadfast love endures forever. We nonetheless learn that Samaria must bear the guilt for rebelling against this loving God, consequently having its pregnant women ripped open and its babies dashed to death (Hosea 13:16).

Hey, guys: if your testicles are injured or your rod cut off, you are commanded not to enter into the congregation of the Lord (Deuteronomy 23:1-2). This is just as well since, in such a case, you probably want to be on the way to the hospital.

Demonstrating a somewhat rare moment of sound mental health, Lord God Yahweh describes Himself as one who is more interested in blotting out our transgressions for His own sake (Isaiah 43:25) than presumably in punishing us. Heaven only knows, the Lord has enough of His own issues to deal with, without choosing to judge us for ours.

One night an angel of the Lord kills 185,000 Assyrian soldiers and these all wake up dead the next morning (2 Kings 19:35). Other than that, it was business as usual except that coffee was no longer available.

After Aaron's two sons, Nadab and Abihu, offer incense to light an "unauthorized fire," the biblical God puts them in the hot seat. Well, it's actually quite a lot worse than that, given that He burns them both alive (Leviticus 10:1-2).

And, in case you missed it in Exodus 22:29, Yahweh wants you to know He is boss and one way He accomplishes this is by making you offer your firstborn to Him in a sacrificial fire (Ezekiel 20:26). The silver lining is, you'll be free to have new children who won't have to be ritualistically murdered.

The fear of the biblical God will lead you to life, satisfaction and freedom from harm (Proverbs 19:23). Beware those New Testament-corrupted deceivers who would have you believe that perfect love casts out all fear (1 John 4:18).

In essence Proverbs 20:30 informs us that physical blows causing wounds cleanse the recipients of evil. While it seems rather far-fetched that beating the crap out of someone specifically accomplishes this, it does have a laxative effect for those who survive the assault.

Chapter Two: A SUPREME BEING NOT QUITE BEYOND COMPARE

"Was the Big Bang nothing more than gastral projection? That would certainly prove the existence of a Supreme Bean."
-- Swami Beyondananda

Whether the biblical God is real or simply represents the dark collective imagination of clueless Bible writers doesn't much matter. Suffice it to say, the man god in the sky of the Judeo-Christian-Islamic tradition simply doesn't pass the smell test when it comes to resembling a being worth worshiping.

Contrary to biblical propaganda, the biblical God is very much short on omnipotence, as you'll see. In fact, waffling is clearly no stranger to His (Ancient of Days) psyche. Quite frankly, we see signs of early dementia in a Being ever so boldly advertised as all-knowing and eternal.

More disturbing is His character. He hands out death sentences like candy, specifically poison candy, and this even includes eternal death sentences. How exactly is it that divine justice is served by punishing souls in infinite measure for even large numbers of finite sins or offenses? Biblical illogic simply knows no rational bounds.

Far from resembling the perfect gift-giving Father of Lights, the biblical God is by his own admission a jealous God and He is chock full of shadow, especially his own Jungian shadow. Quite oddly, it seems to escape requisite attention in Christendom that Yahweh identifies himself as the author, not just of good, but also of evil. In this regard, His image and likeness less conforms to that of the Father of Lights than to the Persian rooster-headed god Abraxas (composite of good and evil) alluded to by Karl Jung, Herman Hesse, and others.

There's undoubtedly something fishy about Exodus 15:3, for there the biblical God identifies himself as a Man-of-War. The official Latin name for this dangerous ocean species is nomeus gronovii, and it is more commonly called a bluebottle.

On Yahweh's command, the Israelites murder many categories of Egypt's firstborn including babies, toddlers, and those objectified animals referred to as livestock (Exodus 12:28-30). Death apparently touches every home in Egypt, causing high demand in the Rx market for anxiety, depression and insomnia medications.

Sometimes Yahweh repents (Exodus 32:14), other times, not (Numbers 23:19). In this regard, the Bible is as clear as mud in helping us understand the confusing, confused nature of the less-than-adorable biblical God we are all called upon to worship and adore.

Yahweh identifies Himself as a jealous God who visits iniquity on children for their parents' sins, even extending to the third or fourth generation (Exodus 20:5). The plot thickens, almost into a paste, as the Lord conversely declares at another time that the sins of the parents are definitely not to be visited on the children (Ezekiel 18:20).

On the first day of creation, the biblical God ostensibly creates light (Genesis 1:3). Oddly enough, it's not till the fourth day that he gets around to creating the sun, moon and stars (Genesis 1:16), perhaps with the aid of a candle or makeshift torch.

The allegedly-omniscient biblical God appears to be pretty much in the dark about the nature of earth's moon (Genesis 1:16), a stellar body which, unlike the sun, reflects rather than generates light. Those who think that shedding light on scriptural ignorance is the devil's work are well advised to think again.

As a reward for doing a kick ass job wrestling with men and even an angel, the biblical God rewards Jacob with a new name, namely "Israel" (Genesis 35:9). But God's being perfect doesn't mean He can't on occasion be forgetful. For example,

Even as the biblical God has a face (Exodus 33:20), He also has a gastrointestinal tract, apparently a rather toxic one. In fact, the Bible tells us that a wind went out from the Lord that caused hundreds of thousands of quails to perish (Numbers 11:31).

The biblical God has hidden himself in a cloud and therefore cannot be reached by prayer (Lamentations 3:44). It can therefore be argued from silence that He had moved His residence to America's Great Pacific Northwest.

Apparently a Blood O type, the biblical God offers instructions to the Israelites on how to sacrifice two young lambs a day to Him (Exodus 29:38-42). Maybe embarrassed by how disgusting animal sacrifice really is, He denies ever having made the request (Jeremiah 7:22), writing it off as fake news.

The biblical God is intimately acquainted with all your ways and scrutinizes you, even when you lie down (Psalm 139:3). Therefore, best to keep your frisky hand to yourself lest the Lord writes you off as a jerk off.

Yahweh is looking to have a house built for Him where He can rest (Isaiah 66:1). Whether this house is to serve as a nursing facility or assisted living facility is not made clear.

The biblical God's eyes are upon you and the Lord thus sees all of man's steps (Job 34:21). For guys who can dance, this no doubt includes the two-step.

Guys, the biblical God is intent upon your severed foreskin serving as a token of the Covenant between you and Him. Since circumcision traumatizes male infants, maybe your parents can talk the Lord into accepting a substitute token, maybe from your local subway system, should it exist.

Spiritualists and mediums are to be put to death, according to the biblical God (Leviticus 20:27). But this doesn't necessarily guarantee that they won't come back to haunt you.

Under the auspice of Roman law and custom, you were free to worship whoever or whatever your heart desired. Unfortunately, under the more tight-ass Mosaic Law, you were to be given a death sentence for worshiping any god but Yahweh (Deuteronomy 17:2-5) or for enticing family members to do the same (Deuteronomy 13:6-10).

The eyes of the Lord are in every place beholding the evil and the good (Proverbs 15:3). But He doesn't just behold these, he also creates them, unfortunately (Isaiah 45:7).

Chapter Three: HARD TO CONCEIVE: THE VIRGIN BIRTH TRAUMA-DRAMA AND ITS MESSIANIC MESS

"My father was Methodist, my mother, Catholic, and I was unplanned. I guess that makes me a rhythm Methodist."
--Swami Beyondananda

Stories of miraculous births of special people are certainly not uncommon in antiquity and this of course includes the stories about Jesus Christ's alleged Virgin Birth. Of course, most of these tales admittedly dwell in the realm of mythology. Unfortunately, regarding the Virgin Birth of Jesus Christ, this is not the case. The Roman Catholic Church and most of the 33,000 other Christian denominations endorse the Virgin Birth as a literal historical event. But it doesn't end there. Based upon the prophet Muhammad's testimony as to its truth, most of the roughly two billion Muslims in the world today accept the veracity of this "miracle." Nonetheless, little evidence exists that the two billion Muslims and 2.2 billion Christians combined openly endorse the literal existence of Santa Claus, the Easter Bunny or the Tooth Fairy, so things really aren't quite as bleak as they at first appear for anyone choosing reality over surreality.

If you were to spend the time doing a parallel rather than chronological reading of the Matthew and Mark accounts of the Virgin Birth and early Jesus story, you'd quickly see that the two accounts vary significantly, and they frankly contradict each other all over the place. Not even the Lord's genealogy can be taken as a given as the two (Matthew's and Luke's) compete for the reader's favor. Whether or not something is or isn't fishy in Denmark, taken literally, the Virgin Birth "miracle" really does stink to high heaven as something astonishingly less than remotely believable. What's more, Jesus Christ Himself specifically warns His followers against trying to build one's faith on signs and wonders, calling it a wicked generation that involves itself in this vain query (Luke 11:29). This hasn't stopped Christianity from building its faith on a literal understanding of the Virgin Birth and also of course on the Resurrection.

Fortunately, there is a way out of this unbelievable silliness, namely, joining the world of esoterica in acknowledging that stories like this are to be perceived symbolically, not literally. Certain of the Christian gnostic texts including The Gospel of Philip attempted to view certain stories as symbolically -- not literally -- true. Never mind that one can convene an assembly of Gnostics (spiritual "knowers") and they'll all give you a different version of the Truth. At least, as friends of symbolic interpretation, they are not tied to a literalism that humanity can ill afford in its quest to move beyond superstition -- a superstition which cynical politicians and the priestcraft is only too happy to exploit

The Apostle Paul, as the earliest writer of New Testament material, seems to space out big time, neglecting to mention anything about Jesus Christ being the fruit of a miraculous Virgin Birth. Paul does, however, demonstrate an astute understanding of human biology, brilliantly informing us that Jesus was "born of a woman" (Galatians 4:4).

There is a genealogical error in the Bible which results in Jesus Christ having two paternal grandfathers in his ancestral chart, Heli (Luke 3:23) and Jacob (Matthew 1:16). If we want to make lemonade out of lemons here, we can at least take solace in knowing that, as a boy, Jesus likely got twice the amount of presents at Hanukkah.

The author of Luke, quite confident that He was on the right track, traces Jesus Christ's genealogy all the way back to Adam. This puts modern day genealogists and their technology to shame.

We learn from Numbers 1:18 that Jewish pedigrees are traced through the father, not the mother. Therefore, the Luke genealogy cannot be that of Jesus Christ's mother Mary since Mary would not have been eligible to sit on the throne of David, only perhaps to dust and polish it.

Christian apologists claim that the Luke genealogy belongs to Mary, not her husband Joseph, even though Mary's name is nowhere shown in the Luke gospel and Joseph's definitely is (Luke 3:23). Hot headed critics who consider these apologists might be involved in what they consider a cover up, often utter expletives like, "Jesus Christ!" and/or "Jesus, Mary and Joseph!"

No less than five biblical passages (2 Samuel 7:12-13, Psalm 132:11, Romans 1:3, Acts 2:30, and 2 Timothy 2:8) inform us that the messiah must be a physical (not just metaphysical) descendant of King David. The alleged Virgin Birth would thus cut Jesus Christ off from His genealogical roots and make His messianic claim null and void.

What is the most likely reason there wasn't any room at the inn for baby Jesus and His parents, Mary and Joseph? It is the stubborn fact that inns, even Holiday Inns, didn't seem to exist at the time.

According to the Luke gospel, Jesus Christ was a descendant of Nathan (Luke 3:31), not Nathan's brother Solomon, the one chosen by the biblical God to be the ancestor of the promised Jewish messiah. In order to be eligible for the throne of David, Jesus would have had to be in the lineage of Solomon (1 Chronicles 29:1).

Isaiah 7:14 actually informs us that a maid or young woman (alma) had conceived or would conceive, depending how the verse is translated. Since the Hebrew word for virgin is betulah, not alma (Genesis 24:43, Exodus 2:8), the general response to a young woman conceiving would likely have been a yawn, maybe followed by the words, "Great, what else is new?"

Even if the author of Isaiah had used the literal word for virgin (betulah) in naming the woman, it still wouldn't have been a big deal, and would certainly not have indicated anything remotely resembling a supernatural event. A woman getting pregnant the first time she has sex is hardly a miracle, especially for virgins who don't passionately insist upon condoms.

At any rate, the much touted story in Isaiah, Chapter 14 doesn't seem to have much of anything to do prophetically with the future Jesus Christ. Read in context, it entirely concerns itself with a royal named King Ahaz, a guy desperate for a miraculous ending to his plight of being imminently overthrown by a confederate alliance threatening his reign.

Before Mary and Joseph came together, Mary was found to be with child (Matthew 1:18). While it's great that the two were found, the Bible makes no mention of where or how they had gotten lost in the first place.

Yes, Mary marvels out loud about how she could possibly be pregnant since she hadn't known a man (Luke 1:34-35). Of course, a lot of women get pregnant without knowing the guy they hook up with and this is why they often end up single moms, the guy proving himself to be a jerk.

Mary and Joseph must have been painfully confused to learn that their Son, the Lord Himself, was to be named Emmanuel (Matthew 1:23). This must have sorely puzzled both spouses, not least because they had already named the kid Joshua (Jesus).

You can be saved solely by calling on the name of Jesus Christ (Acts 4:12) and no other name will do, unless of course you subscribe to Matthew 1:23. Then you might at least consider throwing a Hail Mary pass in trying the name "Emmanuel."

Luke 1:27 mentions Joseph as being from the House of David. The last name of David isn't mentioned, but it's not likely Smith or Jones or even Feinstein.

Mary's cousin Elizabeth was a daughter of Aaron (Luke 1.5), though not former Milwaukee Braves great, Hank Aaron. This would have placed her (and likely Mary as well) squarely or at least obliquely, not in the house of David, but rather that of Levi, the great pants maker.

Apparently being geography-challenged, the author of Matthew declares that the town of Nazareth is in District 23 of the province Galilee (Matthew 2:22). The fact that Nazareth is in Judea, not Galilee, in no way damages the author's purported later claim that Cuba sits 90 miles off the coast of Portugal.

After hearing from the apostle Philip that the Messiah had been located in Nazareth, Nathanael rhetorically barks, "Can anything good come out of Nazareth?" But just for the record, Nazareth was a crappy, little suburb of Capernaum -- one plagued by too much preaching, a lack of decent restaurants and, worst of all, poor sanitation and substandard high school sports teams.

If the so called three "wise men" had, as the Bible claims, followed a star in the east (Matthew 2:2), they'd not have ended up traveling west towards Bethlehem. Be that as it may, a nice visit to Asia wouldn't have been without merit, considering the great dining options there.

If you believe Matthew 1:11, Jesus Christ was a descendant of Coniah (i.e. Jeconiah), a king cursed by Yahweh never to have any of his prodigy sit on the throne of David. What this means is, Jesus Himself was thus ineligible to be the messiah (Jeremiah 36:30), although He no doubt would have made a great philosophy professor.

Christian prophecy buffs argue that Old Testament Mica 5:2 refers to the coming of Jesus Christ, but if this is the case, something is eminently strange since three verses later (Micah 5:5), the claim is made that the individual in question would deliver the Jews from the Assyrians. Now since the Assyrian Empire had ceased to exist some 600 years before the Lord was allegedly born, the best possible explanation is time travel.

Mary's husband Joseph was always dreaming and taking his dreams even more seriously than any self-respecting Jungian analyst might recommend. In one of these many dreams, Joseph is told to arise and flee with Mary and baby Jesus to Egypt, thus avoiding the wrath of King Herod who apparently still wanted to kill the child (Matthew 2:13). In the Luke genealogy, however, Herod was already dead-as-a-doornail by the time of Joseph's dream and, therefore, there would have been no need for any flight to Egypt, not even for a sightseeing vacation to the pyramids or Casino Sharm El Sheikh.

In another dream, an angel commands Joseph to return with Mary and baby Jesus from Egypt. Being afraid of Herod's son Archelaus, who was then ruling, Joseph disobeys, only going as far as Nazareth in Judea. Unable to find a scriptural passage supporting this tale, the Matthew author makes one up, confidently declaring "That it might be fulfilled that was spoken by the prophets, He shall be called a Nazarene." (Matthew 2:23)

The Matthew author claims that Jesus' eventual return from Egypt fulfilled the alleged prophecy of Hosea 11:1 which reads "Out of Egypt I have called my son." If you read the chapter in context, however, the person in question wasn't likely Jesus Christ since, whoever he was, he had a nasty habit of burning incense to graven images while idolatrously sacrificing to the bloodthirsty pagan god Baal.

In Luke 1:47, Mary tells us that her spirit has rejoiced in God her Savior. Why she puts this in the past tense is unclear, but maybe it has something to do with her having to breastfeed and otherwise appease a cranky kid, and to change his dirty diapers.

Chapter Four: PAUL AND PAULINE
CHRISTIANITY

"Hey, Paul! Is that an epistle your packing?"
-- Swami Beyondananda

It has unflatteringly been said of the Apostle Paul, the true founder of Christianity, that those who didn't know him, revered him while those who did know him thought he was a total jerk. Regardless, this prolific egotist feigning to be a saint is certainly the most influential personage in the history of Christianity, with the possible exception of Jesus Christ. We do know that Paul never had the pleasure of meeting Jesus in the flesh. We also know that Paul had almost nothing to say about the "historical Jesus." In fact, religious historian extraordinaire Dr. Bart Ehrman makes the fascinating point that the info Paul shares about the man Jesus would easily fit on one side of a 3 x 5 index card.

As proud author of at least seven of the epistles (letters) attributed to him, Paul did more than any of the other apostles to get Christian theology and its salvation-obsessed bandwagon rolling. While the so called Pastorals (Titus, and both 1 and 2 Timothy) have now been conclusively written off as plagiarisms, it's still debated whether or not the same is the case with Ephesians, Colossians, and 2 Thessalonians. What's not debated is the fact that Paul really did write Romans, Galatians, Philippians, 1 Thessalonians, Philemon, and both 1 and 2 Corinthians. Paul did not, however, write 3 Corinthians, a highly amusing and bemusing, if disturbing, epistle that never made the canonical cut. It's there we learn the truth about the early agape love feasts, events that have been falsely romanticized by people not lacking in either hindsight or heinie sight. We read in 3 Corinthians that on designated feast days, wealthy Christians would get to the feasts quite early and proceed to drink most all the wine and eat most of the food before their working class brethren (mostly slaves) had even arrived!

For our purposes, sorting out authorship of the 13 Pauline Epistles is much less important than what is actually communicated therein; in fact, in the modern age, pretty much no one cares who wrote what. We'll therefore not bother further distinguishing authorship as we have some fun with the material itself, going on faith that a global family that plays and wordplays together, stays together. Hopefully, this section will not cast a pall.

Before his conversion, the Apostle Paul was apparently complicit in the apprehension, persecution and even murder of Christians including that of Stephen (Acts 8:1-2). Nonetheless, the Apostle boldly declares himself entirely innocent of the shedding of all blood (Acts 20:26), perhaps showing the first signs of early dementia.

In the world of Pauline Christianity, slaves were to show full respect for their masters, so as not to shame the biblical God and His teachings (1Timothy 6:1-2). It didn't seem to occur to the author or even to the Christian-indoctrinated American Confederacy that slavery itself is what's shameful.

The Apostle Paul's mention of the spiritual gift of "divers kinds of tongues" (1 Corinthians 12:10) is best not dwelt upon or taken any-too-seriously. It's uncommon for divers to speak in tongues, or even without them, while engaged in underwater threats of often oceanic proportions.

Paul wants you to get a circumcision of the heart (Romans 2:29). If you have heart trouble, however, you might generally prefer to go with angioplasty or maybe a bypass.

According to 1 Thessalonians 4:16, the Lord is going to descend from heaven with a shout. It remains unclear, however, who or what He might be shouting at or about what.

According to First Corinthians 11:3, the head of every man is Christ, and the head of the woman is man. Be that as it may, according to Paul, the point can logically be made that women with men's heads aren't particularly attractive to some of us, especially heterosexual males.

Paul claims that it is shameful for men to have long hair (1 Corinthians 11:14). But since there are many women who love guys with long hair, these guys could generally care less about Paul's opinion on the matter, not least because they are often getting laid abundantly.

While you women are generally not well regarded in the Bible, you can apparently be saved from eternal damnation, compliments of child bearing (1 Timothy 2:15). The good news is, if you choose eternal hell over the hell of child bearing, you'll almost certainly have a more fulfilling social life and a helluva lot more personal time while here on earth, the alleged future be damned.

Never mind the praise Paul has historically received for saying, "I die daily" (1 Corinthians 15:31). This naive admission made the apostle an automatic decline for any and all empire life insurance offerings.

According to Paul, there is only one who receives the prize in the race (1 Corinthians 9:24). Unfortunately, this is an error of Olympian proportions, given that, in his obsession with the gold,

Paul forgot the bronze and silver, and especially the sweet, empathetic magic of the Special Olympics in which everyone wins for a blessed change.

Paul claims that all athletes are disciplined in their training (1 Corinthians 9:25). This can only mean the Apostle had no foreknowledge of the NFL's Cleveland Browns who went 0-16 in 2017 and have had similar seasons since their haunted founding in the year of our Lord,1944.

Paul admits robbing other churches in order to benefit the Church at Corinth (2 Corinthians 11:8). If the Church of Rome happened to be among Paul's defrauded victims, what we have here is a clear case of the opportunistic Apostle robbing Peter to pay Paul.

In Acts 20:25, Paul is said to have acknowledged that those standing there would never see his face again. Since so many folks considered Paul a control freak and a jerk, this was likely less of a problem than the narcissistic Apostle might have vainly imagined.

In Romans 2:20, Paul instructs the faithful to feed their enemies as part of a grand strategy designed to "heap burning coals on their heads." At the end of the day, even plain old heartburn sounds much, much better by comparison.

According to Paul, Christians are bought by Jesus Christ with a price (1 Corinthians 6:20). Based upon the appalling behavior of many who call themselves Christians, we can only hope that Jesus received a well-deserved discount.

The Bible speaks enthusiastically of the election of God (1 Thessalonians 1:4). Whether or not the Lord just won the Electoral College or the popular vote as well remains frustratingly unclear.

Paul boasts about all the calamities he has suffered in service to Christ, and this includes getting stoned at least once (2 Corinthians 11: 23-33). Be that as it may, Paul's politically-incorrect mention of smoking weed ought never have made it into the pages of sacred scripture, disturbing as this is.

Paul had to have been really stoned when he declared that Jesus Christ was first to rise from the dead (Acts 26:23). The Bible does in fact mention three earlier resurrections, namely those found in 1 Kings 17:17-22, 2 Kings 4:23-35, 2 Kings 13:20-21, although no one asked that these other resurrected souls be regarded as the Savior.

Contrary to the claim in Ephesians 5:14, the author of Isaiah doesn't say anything in Chapter 9, Verse 2 about the resurrection of the dead nor does he identify the perceived light in question as that of Christ. The light might just as easily have been from a 4th of July fireworks display or a UFO.

Want to talk about a really serious drinking problem for Christians, one much worse than cases simply involving alcohol? If you drink the blood of Christ in an unworthy state, you'll be eternally damned (1 Corinthians 11:29), and to add insult to severe injury, your taste buds will likely be pissed off at you for what may seem like an eternity.

Paul wasn't sheepish about claiming that a Christian woman's choice was to cover her head or be shorn (1 Corinthians 11:6). In spite of the sheer humiliation of this, the violated woman could at least take (minor) comfort in her (presumed) empathetic identification with the sheep of Christ (John 10:16).

The advice given in Ephesians 6:18 is to pray always with all prayer. This is apparently to be distinguished from one's praying sometimes with some prayer or even for the Zen koan-friendly praying sometimes with no prayer.

It is Roman procurer Portius Festus (no relation to the Addams Family's Uncle Fester) who arranges for Paul to go to Rome to stand trial. The end result is that Paul quite literally loses his head in a sharp dispute with the Roman Empire.

If you think it prudent to put on all of God's armor (Ephesians 6:11) and if it happens to be during the full heat of summer, don't forget to wear lots of deodorant. Otherwise, you'll likely risk severe olfactory rebuke from the rest of the Body of Christ.

It's all well and good that, according to Paul, the eye can never say to the hand, "I don't need you" (1 Corinthians 12:21). This is especially true when you are engaged in the pleasurable monkey business of auto-eroticism.

The tenth of the Ten Commandments concerns itself with not coveting people, place or thing when it comes to your neighbor. While Paul is okay with this at least to a point, the Apostle would argue that coveting life's best gifts is apparently a desirable exception to the rule (1 Corinthians 12:31).

We are told in 1Timothy 3:2-3 that wine is a mocker and strong drink rages. Therefore, if you get pulled over for drinking and driving, and happen to get testy with the arresting officer, be sure to tell her it was the wine, not you, that mouthed off.

In 2 Corinthians 2:1, Paul writes: "But I determined this with myself, that I would not come again to you in heaviness." This can only mean that Paul was intent on losing some serious weight.

Chapter Five: DARK SIDE OF THE BRIGHT AND MORNING STAR

Q. Swami, will I burn in hell?
A. Not if you use #48 sunscreen. You'll get a great tan.
-- Swami Beyondananda

Never mind that no small number of Christians think of Jesus Christ, not only as God (the Second Person of the Trinity), but also as a great guy, someone you'd love to have a beer with and discuss family felicity and world peace. But wait a minute - not so fast!

The truth that helps set these folks nervously free is that no less than 70 of the 162 verses in the Bible specifically dealing with the lovely topic of eternal hell are allegedly authored by Jesus Christ Himself. And this really shouldn't come as a surprise since the convoluted "Prince of Peace" and aspiring Hurdy Gurdy Man love child from Palestine is on biblical record saying that He actually hadn't come to bring peace but rather the sword (Matthew 10:34). What's more, from the Lord's perspective, hell is not to be taken metaphorically, but literally, and if you're not part of the born again Christian tribe, you are the equivalent of an accursed goat doomed to enter the everlasting fire (Matthew 25:41), and probably without the benefit of Blistex or even an air conditioning unit.

Unfortunately, the dark art of controlling people through the fear of hell has historically been no more a stranger to religion than to politics, and has in fact achieved its greatest hellish successes in the convergence of politics and religion, especially those convergences with an aspiring theocratic bent.

If you read the Bible in an analytical manner, it will be hard to deny that, at least in one major portrayal, Jesus Christ is a highly motivated theocratic politician, one seeking His own egoic reward here on earth as He would also have it in heaven. Blasphemous as it may sound to the minds and emotions of the faithfully pre-programmed, this particular Jesus is embarrassingly pseudo-humble and is actually full of Himself in a way that can leave the discerning reader incredulous. What's more, this Jesus is terribly unkind and incredibly insensitive. And yes, He is even willing to threaten non-compliant beings, not only with spiritual death, but perhaps even murder here on earth. And no, this is definitely not a guy you'd want to have a beer with!

Jesus Christ wants you to take His yoke upon yourself and be taught by Him because, according to his testimony, He is humble and gentle at heart, and you will find rest for your soul by doing so (Matthew 11:29). Shortly thereafter, perhaps under the influence of wine, the Lord raises eyebrows by uninhibitedly referring to Himself as One greater than the Temple (Matthew 12:6).

Jesus Christ is meek and lowly of heart (Matthew 11:29) and He doesn't seek his own glory (John 8:50). The day comes, however, when the Lord is stuffed to the Piscean Age gills with the humble pie diet and, and speaking of Himself in the third person, boldly declares: "The hour has come for the Son to be glorified" (John 12:23).

One way the Lord seeks His own glory is to let His friend Lazarus die, so that He, Jesus Christ, could raise Him from the dead (John

11:1-44) and presumably receive a standing ovation. And the Church said 'Amen'?

In John 8:58 the biblical Jesus tells us: "Before Abraham was, I Am." This didn't necessarily go over well with the Jews who didn't collectively believe that God could be a farting, defecating mammal, and so the primal church Christians began marketing their message to certain among the often more gullible pagans, finally succeeding brilliantly.

Jesus Christ tells critics that if a certain crowd loudly worshiping him as King were to fall quiet, then the very stones along the road would burst into cheers (Luke 19:39-40). If this could have been pulled off, especially while combining baritone, tenor, and base, it would have been all for the symphonic good, better, best.

Jesus Christ is a very busy guy, not only being the way, the truth and the life, but also creation's only gateway to the Father (John 14:6). Presumably this gateway is closed during non-working hours and when the Lord is on vacation, so do yourself a huge favor and time your death accordingly.

It may have been riskier than you think for Jesus Christ to have repeatedly referred to himself in the third person as "the son of man". Alarmingly, Psalm146:3 cautions the discerning to trust neither princes nor the son of man (in whom there is no help), and Job 25:6 gets downright gross, referring to both man and the son of man as worms, though not specifically as parasites.

When Jesus Christ unexpectedly says that the Father is greater than He (John 14:28), it's not likely concerning the biblical God's weight. As far as we know, no one seems to have put the First or Second Persons of the Trinity on the scales.

Jesus Christ also wants you to know that all of the world teachers who came before him were thieves and robbers (John 10:80). Aside from the fact it's not explained what is the difference between a thief and a robber, there's the problem of Jesus wittingly or unwittingly discrediting all the Israelite prophets of bygone ages.

Don't be deceived into believing you can keep your life once you find it, the truth being, you can only find and keep it permanently by losing it for Jesus Christ's sake (Matthew 16:25). Of course, losing anything including one's life can best be prevented by paying attention to where you put it in the first place.

If you deny Jesus Christ before God, He's going to deny you before His Heavenly Father (Matthew 10:33). The silver lining is, if He denies you after the Father rather than before, it will buy you a little more time to party hardy in the tantalizing flesh.

On the one hand, the only real choice any of us have is to repent or face soul damnation (Luke 13:3). On the other hand, it's really only one out of a hundred persons who has any real need to repent (Luke 15:7), so apparently the rest can just chill, not worrying about any uncomfortable overheating scenarios in hell.

If people are superior to other mammals such as sheep, as Jesus Christ argues (Matthew 12:12), then it might have been better for the Lord not to have repeatedly referred to his followers as the woolly, bleating same. It's irritating enough to make one want to get the Lord's proverbial goat.

Jesus Christ is not fooling around when he says that if you as much as call your brother a fool, you are in danger of hellfire ((Matthew 5:22). If you disregard the Lord's warning, perhaps He will be your bunk mate in hell inasmuch as He Himself liberally, relentlessly attacks others as fools (Luke 11:40, Matthew 23:17-19).

On good days of the week, Jesus Christ advises His faithful to love their enemies and bless those who curse them (Matthew 5:44). Unfortunately, the Lord goes just a little off script sometimes, calling His own enemies blind fools, hypocrites, vipers, and whited sepulchers (Matthew 23:17).

Jesus Christ demonstrates profound respect for the Fourth Commandment He so often preached (Honor your parents). For example, the Lord (who may not be coming to your future funeral) tells a guy who wants to follow Him, but first needs to bury his newly deceased father: "Let the dead bury the dead." (Matthew 8:22)

Jesus Christ blissfully informs His would-be converts that, in order to follow him, it's entirely necessary to hate your parents and the rest of your friggin' family (Luke 14:26). There's no doubt that for more than a few folks, this is a veritable cakewalk, one requiring no effort whatsoever.

Matthew 21:18-22 conveniently spares us the devil-in-the-details regarding the fig tree cursed and killed by Jesus Christ, the one that, quite logically, wasn't capable of bearing fruit out of season. The good news is, there's no mention anywhere in the New Testament of the Lord having dealt in similar fashion with a prepubescent goat incapable of providing Him milk-on-demand.

In a display of abusive mystical power that would have shocked PETA and other animal rights groups, Jesus Christ accedes to the request of demons to possess a herd of roughly 2,000 pigs. The unfortunate pigs, apparently written off by the Lord as collateral damage, subsequently rush down a steep embankment and are drowned in a lake below (Mark 5:1-17).

We know from scripture that the Prophet Elijah mass murdered 450 unarmed prisoners at Kishon Brook (1 Kings 18:40) and that Moses, among a slew of other atrocities, ordered the massacre of 3,000 family and friends (Exodus 32:28). Undeterred by bad press, both these guys eventually show up for a transfiguring chat and timeless photo op with Jesus Christ up on Mt. Tabor (Matthew 17:3).

In a thinly veiled parable (Luke 19:27), Jesus Christ commands that all those who don't accept him as king be rounded up, brought before him, and executed. It's not hard to see why Imperial Rome didn't buy the Lord's flimsy argument that His kingdom was not of this world.

If you live inside Jesus Christ, you cannot commit sin (1 John 3:6). It will nonetheless be dark in there and a little hard to move around.

Chapter Six: JESUS CHRIST: THE BREAD OF LIFE OR HARD-TO-DIGEST STEW?

"The bread of life is best leavened with levity."
-- Swami Beyondananda

Jesus Christ is many things to many people, but that doesn't mean He is always on top of being the Lord, God or being perfect as His Father in heaven supposedly is (Matthew 5:48). There are those day to day bothersome things that he just has trouble tracking, including some of the basics of daily life like common sense safety when it comes to respecting the hazards of fire, as you'll see. Likewise, the Lord offers some advice that seems to lack even a minimal understanding of nutrition, which can't be great news to health-friendly church bodies like the Seventh Day Adventists.

Jesus Christ has other human flaws as well, like not quite remembering who to credit for some of his lines. And, of course, there's that old favorite - not always practicing what He preached, especially when it comes to being genuinely loving. Sometimes Jesus Christ sounds more than a little like a laid back hippie-type Cynic philosopher, but it's clear from Mark 3:21 that Jesus' family clearly thought He was nuts.

In any case, as you'll see or continue seeing, the notion of Jesus Christ as the bread of life rather than as a hard-to-digest stew is a stretch - a really big stretch capable of dislocating numerous mythic joints in the Body of Christ. Ready to help bust the *myth* labs?

The Bible tells us that the Lord is God and there is none beside Him (Deuteronomy 4:35). Therefore, best to ignore 1 Peter 3:22 which claims that Jesus can now be located in heaven on God's right side.

Even though all power has ostensibly been given to Jesus Christ in heaven and on earth (John 3:35), He nonetheless remains powerless to decide who will sit on his right and left hand (Matthew 20:23). Of course having someone sit on either hand wouldn't be all that comfortable under any circumstances.

Hiding a candle under a bushel (Matthew 5:15) would potentially be as dangerous today as it was in Jesus' Christ's day, given that, under certain conditions, agricultural products like wheat are extremely flammable and, if lit, could burn a house down, not just toast marshmallows. It's all well and good to accept Jesus as your personal Lord and Savior, but maybe not your fire marshal.

Jesus Christ wants you to know that there's nothing that you can take in from the outside that can or will defile you (Mark 7:15). What clearer proof do you need that the Lord never ate at McDonald's?

The Son of Man is coming with His angels in the glory of His Father and He will repay every person for what he or she has done (Matthew 16:27). Once this occurs, Jesus will hopefully be debt-free and thus able to relax more fully.

Whether or not heaven really is like a grain of mustard seed, as Jesus Christ alleges (Matthew 13:31,32), is a moot point. The Lord would not likely have made a good gardener or botanist given that in the above-referenced passage, He errs no less than 3 times in claiming that the mustard seed is the smallest of all seeds, grows into the largest of all plants, and finally becomes a tree.

Apparently, if you have faith even as small as a mustard seed, you can order a mulberry tree to uproot itself and then replant itself in the sea (Luke 17:6). Nonetheless, it won't likely grow very well in its new location nor will the proverbial monkey have much success in chasing the weasel unless both are on water skis.

Evidently irritated, Jesus Christ addresses the apostle Peter, saying "Get thee behind me, Satan." One would think that strategically, the Lord would have been better served by having Satan out front where He could keep an eye on him.

There's ostensibly a demoniac spirit, a so called deaf-and-dumb one, who is quite well versed in the art of reading lips. Upon verbal command from Jesus Christ, this spirit immediately obeys the Lord, exiting the body of the man he had pissed off by demonically possessing his body temple (Mark 9:25-26) without bothering to pay rent.

Jesus Christ deploys his significant gift of healing, making a woman who has been bent over for eighteen years, straight again (Luke 13:11-16). Thus began the long evolution of chiropractic medicine.

Jesus Christ informs us that if we try to save our lives, we'll lose them, but if we lose our lives for His sake and the gospel's, we'll save them (Mark 8:35). This is remarkably astute of the Lord, given that the gospels had not yet come to exist.

According to Jesus Christ, the one unforgivable sin is blasphemy against the Holy Spirit (Matthew 12:31-32). But since unforgiveness itself, being the opposite of forgiveness, is logically unforgivable, there must be at least two unforgivable sins, one of these being unforgiveness itself.

We know that Jesus Christ has His own house (Mark 2:15). Is it that the Lord was a hoarder and the house so cluttered, He had no place to lay His head and therefore envied even foxes living in holes (Matthew 8:20)?

According to Jesus Christ, the way one enters into eternal life is by keeping five of the Ten Commandments and giving away one's possessions (Matthew 19:16-20). Hey, it's a start!

Did Jesus Christ really say that it's better to give than to receive (Acts 20:35)? If so, it may not be unreasonable to conjecture He was speaking of trash talking or maybe even Rolfing.

Perhaps a bit bored with His own teachings, Jesus Christ takes a quick break. Astonishingly, we find him quoting a line from Aesop's Fables, namely that of the Fisherman Piping: "We piped unto you and you haven't danced." (Matthew 11:17)

Never mind Jesus Christ says He will be with you always till the end of the world (Matthew 28:20). The fact is, by His own admission, He won't (Matthew 26:11). And what's more, where He's going, you can't even go (John 7:34), bummer.

So, Jesus Christ speaks in parables so that people will see without seeing and hear without hearing (Luke 8:10)? Parable-babble aside, the same can be achieved by going to your average American party and freely mingling.

Jesus Christ tells us that if you believe in Him, then out of your belly shall flow rivers of living water (John 7:38). Please consider the fact that this may be especially helpful for those believers in need of a really good diuretic.

In Matthew 24:35 Jesus Christ informs us that, even though heaven and earth will pass away, His words won't. But the question necessarily arises, in the conspicuous absence of both heaven and earth, where might the Lord's words be put for safe keeping?

Since Christ suffered physical pain, you had better do the same and if you dedicate the suffering to the Lord, you'll be finished with sin (1 Peter 4:1). Converted to the practices of B &D/S & M, this no doubt gives Christian bottoms a running start in experiencing oodles of pleasurable pain and painful pleasure.

Jesus Christ informs us that marriage will be a thing of the past in the world to come (Matthew 22:30). On the bright side, this means you'll no longer be forced to run the risk of divorce court and alimony payments or be subject to the boredom inherent in territorial monogamy.

The designation "son of God" was nothing divine in the world of first century Jews. We're told in 2 Samuel 7:14, for example, that if any son of God in question sins, he'll be corrected with a good, old-fashioned beating.

Wherever two or three gather in Jesus Christ's name, there He is in the midst of them (Matthew 18:20). Therefore, if you are praying alone in your closet (Matthew 6:6), it may be best to come out and try to get the Lord's attention by finding at least one person to join your fellowship.

Jesus Christ wants you to know that for the benefit of His sheep, there are many mansions in heaven (John 14:2). Frankly, those sheep who are house broken will likely be awarded with the best accommodations.

You can only be saved by calling on the name of Jesus Christ (Acts 4:12). No other name will do unless of course you believe Matthew 1:23 and then you can give the name "Emmanuel" a shot, maybe after a drink or two.

Perhaps desperate for the attention He likely believed He deserved, Jesus Christ tells us that we will die in our sins if we don't believe He is who He claims to be (John 8:24). Did anyone dare retort, "It's all about you, Lord, isn't it?

You're going to need to be ready moment-to-moment for the Second Coming, especially since the Son of Man will be arriving when least expected (Matthew 24:44). If you're suffering insomnia on account of this, you're definitely not alone.

Chapter Seven: CHRISTIANITY'S CRAZY PASSION TALE: WHAT'S THE STORY HERE?

"You say, a scapegoat AND a sacrificial lamb? I say, "BAAA!""
-- Swami Beyondananda

Jesus Christ cordially, simultaneously serves as both a scapegoat and sacrificial lamb. The proverbial scapegoat is one who suffers the herniating burden of the tribes' sins being transferred onto him as he is heckled, then ceremoniously booted out of camp. The sacrificial lamb, on the other hand, is given even a worse deal, being slain, in Jesus' case, for the sins of the world.

Of course, even as Judaism features the bad psychology of the scapegoat routine, it has no place in its theology for a human mammal's wiping out humanity's sins by allowing itself to be murdered. The attempted sacrificial murder by Abraham of his son Isaac may be dear to the hearts of certain Jews, but Isaac's demise would not have taken away the sins of the world. Rather, it would merely have placated the emotional needs of a tribal God seeking a version of absolute, and absolutely dreadful, obedience.

Interestingly, in at least one story written in the Hebrew Talmud, Isaac actually is sacrificially slain by his dad and it is only Isaac's spirit that comes back down the mountain! There's also the horrifying biblical tale of the Israelite warrior Jepthah who does end up killing his child as a sacrifice to God (Judges 11:39) and without as much as a whispered protest from on high. But again, it's not that the daughter's death was intended to take away the sins of the world. This special kookiness is reserved for the domain of Christianity and the pagan myths from which it derives its dark power.

Even if you happen to have bought into the story that you are saved from eternal damnation by the blood of the slain and resurrected Lamb, Jesus Christ, serious problems still haunt the theological scene. For example, the four New Testament authors, code name Matthew, Mark, Luke and John, don't seem to agree on hardly any of the details of Jesus Christ's death including who might have witnessed it, and who was present at the crucifixion or empty tomb. There's also a disagreement among the big four on the time of Jesus Christ's death and, believe it or not, even the day.

At first glance, it appears that the Mark and John authors are in agreement on the day. As you dig into the two gospel stories, wrestling with the pesky devils in the details, you'll be hard pressed not to notice that in the John version, the Lord actually is slain on the Day of Preparation of the Passover, whereas in Mark, He survives that day, being crucified the next!

This brings up an important point: why would you stake your alleged salvation on a story that can't even agree on the day Jesus Christ died? It frankly seems like there are better ways to go.

The guy mentioned in Jeremiah 11:19 is apparently like a lamb who is led to the slaughter, not even knowing that his enemies are trying to kill him. This can't possibly be Jesus Christ since the

Lord was more like a fox, cunningly outsmarting and eluding these jerks wherever possible, and even turning tail and slipping away on occasion (John 10:39).

While Matthew 26:21 and Mark 14:18 both say that the presence of Jesus Christ's betrayer (Judas) was revealed during the Last Supper, Luke 22:14-21 claims it was revealed shortly thereafter. Can we just split the difference and say it happened during dessert?

In John 19:6, we find Pontius Pilate allowing the Jews to instigate the brutal torture and crucifixion of Jesus Christ on account of the fact that he, Pilate, found no fault in Him. Can you imagine the Lord's' fate had Pilate actually found fault?

Matthew 27:28 says that the robe Jesus Christ was made to wear by his Roman captors was scarlet, whereas the author of John says it was purple (John 19:2). How about we just agree it was scarlet with purple trim?

In Mark 8:34 Jesus Christ advises you to deny yourself, picking up your cross and following Him. Inasmuch as the Lord hadn't even been arrested yet, let alone sentenced to crucifixion, we can safely assume he expected his followers to be well versed in reading tea leaves.

Scourging and otherwise torturing Jesus Christ, or even forcing Him to put on a purple robe prior to His being convicted of treason (John 19:1-3) would have been completely illegal under Roman law. Never mind that interfacing with historical reality has never been the strong suit of the Christian faith.

If Isaiah 53:5 is speaking prophetically of Jesus Christ, the author apparently specializes in the power of understatement. It's not simply that "the Lord was wounded and bruised" for our iniquities. He was savagely crucified to death by the Romans.

The psalmist (allegedly Jesus Christ) who is speaking in Psalm 69:21 (i.e. the so called vinegar verse) tells us that his enemies gave him gall to eat and vinegar to drink. But far from loving these enemies, the Lord expresses, among other hateful things, a desire to see them blinded (vs. 23) and their homes destroyed (vs. 25), although there's no mention of His trying to get them audited by the IRS.

The claim is made in Matthew 27:35 that the voice of the fellow speaking in Psalm 22:18 is prophetically that of the future Jesus Christ who is apparently talking about lots being cast for his garments at his crucifixion. But since the same guy just twelve verses earlier had referred to himself as a worm (Psalm 22:6), it's unlikely his wardrobe would have had anything in common with the Lord's.

In attempting to prophetically identify the person mentioned in Psalm 72:4, Christian apologists are hard pressed to explain how it could be that the Lord "crushed the oppressor." If it's anything, death by crucifixion is oppressive, not victoriously impressive.

Is Isaiah 53:10 a prophetic reference to Jesus Christ, as Christian apologists claim? Probably not inasmuch as, far from pleasure fructifying in the Lord's hands, the hands themselves were secured to a cruel Roman cross along with his feet.

While hanging from the cross at Golgotha, Jesus Christ was purportedly given a combination of gall and vinegar to drink (Matthew 27:34) or maybe it was wine mixed with myrrh (Mark 15:23) or it might have been vinegar only (John 19:29). Whatever the case, no one is claiming it was a much needed double shot of Sunset Rum or Pincer Vodka.

At the moment Jesus Christ gives up his spirit while hanging from the cross, weird things begin to happen including tombs breaking open and the dead being resurrected (Matthew 27:51). Although unreported, the former dead no doubt all grab a quick shower and a change of clothing before informing the beneficiaries of their life insurance policies that there might be a bit of a problem.

Jesus Christ's prophetically-oriented math skills have been questioned by the faithless and here's why: since Jesus allegedly died on Friday afternoon and was resurrected either late Saturday night or early Sunday morning, the claim of his rising after three days (Matthew 27:63, Mark 8:31) would have meant the Lord finally showed up on Monday, no doubt apologetically.

A careful or even quasi- careful reading of the gospels of John and Mark shows that the two authors don't agree on which day Jesus Christ died, the Day of Preparation of the Passover or the day after. Problematic as this may seem in terms of biblical credibility, it hasn't even slightly slowed down Christian storytellers intent on pushing their myth of biblical consistency.

Displaying a miraculous penchant for handing money, even blood money, Jesus Christ's betrayer Judas buys a field with the 30 pieces of silver (Acts 1:18), but also somehow returns the silver to the priests (Matthew 27:3-5). It can thus be argued that this miraculous feat rivals that of Jesus Christ's multiplying loaves and fishes!

The notion of Jesus Christ as sacrificial lamb being purposed to take away the sins of the world through blood atonement (John 1:29,35) would have been entirely alien to the First Century Jewish mind. In Judaism, only those mammals which had split hooves and which chewed cud were considered eligible for sacrifice, and so it's hard to see how Jesus, a non-cud chewing fellow conspicuously missing split hooves, could have qualified.

The notion that there cannot be any atonement without the shedding of blood (Hebrews 9:22) is spectacularly suspect, and here's why: even if the doctrine of atonement were true, you can successfully atone for your sins through prayer (Hosea 14:3), jewelry (Numbers 31:50), flour (Leviticus 5:11-13), or even money (Exodus 30:15), not including Bitcoin.

Since flour was an acceptable sacrifice (Leviticus 5:11-13), a great opportunity was missed in Jesus Christ's tragic case. In lieu of pushing the Lord's sacrificial crucifixion, everyone could have just pitched in to make, bake, and serve a delicious pizza. They could then throw a party which would have hopefully included beer.

Had at least one hand each been free, the thieves hanging on crosses on either side of Jesus Christ (Matthew 27:38, Mark 15:27) would no doubt have scratched their heads, wondering what the hell they were doing up there? Theft was definitely not a capital offense under Roman law at the time.

Christian prophecy buffs may claim that the individual identified in Isaiah 53:12 as the so called "suffering servant" is Jesus Christ, even though the person mentioned is said not to be strong. Given that Jesus had allegedly been given power over all flesh (John 17:2), it can likely be surmised He was at least strong enough.

In a conversation with Joseph of Arimathea, Roman Prelate Pontius Pilate marvels that it only took Jesus Christ three hours to die (Mark 15:44). This marveling is certainly understandable, given that death-by-crucifixion normally took at least two or three days, which no doubt seemed like an eternity to the victims.

Matthew 28:9 tells us that Mary Magdalene knew Jesus Christ when He first appeared to her after being resurrected, whereas John 20:14 says, no, she didn't at first have a clue who He was. In the spirit of blessed conflation, can we just say that the Lord looked vaguely familiar to Mary?

Mary Magdalene was apparently allowed to touch Jesus Christ when He first appeared to her (Matthew 28:9) although John 20:17 says she was not. Since touching someone you might not at first recognize could be considered impolite, let's go with John's version, okay?

Even if Jesus Christ did rise again from the dead (1 Thessalonians 4:14), He still loses to the Greek god Dionysus (the Thrice Born) by a score of 3-2. Those damn Greeks!

The claim is made in the 27th chapter of Matthew that Judas' betrayal of Jesus Christ for 30 pieces of silver somehow fulfilled Jeremiah 32:6. Unfortunately, the number of shekels involved in that story is seventeen, not thirty, and has absolutely nothing to do with Judas Iscariot's blood money betrayal, but instead focuses on a guy named Hanameel, who is entirely happy with the real estate deal he makes and was likely high fiving everyone.

The claim that Jesus Christ was hanged from a tree (Acts 5:30) makes some Christian fundamentalist literalists quite cross. This is entirely understandable since Deuteronomy 21:23 clearly states: "Cursed is he who hangs on a tree."

While Luke 23:49, Matthew 27:55-56 and Mark 15:40 all claim that the female devotees of Jesus Christ viewed his crucifixion from afar, John 19:25 begs to differ, claiming it was up close and personal. Since eye glasses and contacts had yet to be invented, we can speculatively chalk this discrepancy up to a case of nearsightedness vs. farsightedness.

There's no less than a total of nine alleged resurrections from the dead in the pages of the Bible, that of Eutychus of Troas' being the final one (Acts 20:7-12). It's unlikely that anyone has of late asked you to accept Eutychus or Lazarus as your personal Lord and savior, right?

It was still dark when Jesus' female companions visited the tomb (John 20:1). On the other hand, it wasn't that dark at all since the sun was apparently just then rising (Mark 16:2), and this may shed a whole new light on things. Luke 24:2 informs us that Jesus Christ's tomb was open, whereas Matthew 28:12 says it was closed. This clearly presents us with an open and shut case of it being open or closed.

There were two angels at the tomb (John 20:11-12) or maybe there was just a single angel (Matthew 28:2). If the angel was single, the Bible is mum on whether or not he finally met a compatible female angel and tied the knot.

Matthew 28:3 says that the angel was outside the tomb which is where he'd have to be if the tomb was closed (Matthew 28:1-2); otherwise, he might have suffered claustrophobia. The other three Gospel writers say that the two angels (John 20:1 1-12) or two men

(Luke 24:4) or a young man (Mark 16:5) were inside, and so it can therefore be argued from silence that none were taking a pee break.

Chapter 8: ADDITIONAL BIBLICAL "MIRACLES" TO PONDER

"During the drought in California a few years ago, you wouldn't believe how many people were praying for Jesus to come and turn wine into water."
-- Swami Beyondananda

Assuming Jesus Christ actually existed, he apparently performed no small number of impressive paranormal healings. Of course other "miracle" workers including Simon Magus and Apollonius of Tyanna are said to have done the same. First century Christians embarrassingly stooped really low in attributing the successes of pagan rivals to demoniac power. And isn't it usually this way? As human beings, we have to insist on our own brand being the best or even the only brand, while discrediting those of others.

Over time, as belief in miracles settled in, so has the ugly politics of hypnotizing believers into taking these extremely seriously, even to the extent of staking one's salvation on the alleged miracles' veracity. This would be a much tougher sell were our species a bit more honest. In any case, through a gigantic game of Telephone, one spanning millennial time while sloppily traversing several languages and cultures, Jesus Christ in essence became Jesus Christ superstar, a legendary guy who was far more than just human, in fact, both man and God.

One of the most astonishing things about Christianity is its refusal to distinguish between the tremendous discrepancies presented in the Gospel writers' various portrayals of Jesus. Take for example, the gospel of John vs. the three synoptic gospels of Matthew, Mark and Luke. In the synoptic gospels, Jesus Christ is largely reticent about informing people of His having performed miracles and of displaying "signs and wonders". J.C. even goes so far as to lambast as degenerate, a generation seeking after signs and wonders. In other words, in expressing humility to some degree, He was "just saying no" to the consciousness of building a religion on the sandy soil of miracle-mongering.

Unfortunately for Christians and now the rest of us, J.C.'s modesty over his ability to foster signs, wonders, and miracles wasn't a big seller among the Jews whom the first Christians, being Jews themselves, were trying to win over. If somehow they had been won over, Christianity as a religion would have been more easily contained, the fire being limited to Judaism. But as the ancient world turned, the Jews really did turn out to be a very hard sell, not least because miracles listed in the Tanakh or so called Old Testament were pretty much a dime a dozen. An even bigger deal breaker was Jesus Christ's lack of qualifications as the Jewish messiah. That flunked him and his bogus claim.

Along comes the last of the four gospels, namely, the Gospel of John, which was written soon after it became clear that the Jews were a crappy target audience and enough time, energy and shekels had been wasted on them. The Jesus Christ of the John gospel is hardly shy when it comes to advertising His signs and wonders to the sound of loud applause, or even claiming to be equal with God. The John portrayal of Jesus Christ (the alleged I Am) is really quite pagan, even having the main character turn water into wine at a wedding feast. Unlike the Jesus Christ of the synoptic gospels, John's Jesus deploys

the paranormal as a marketing means for creating faith. In the synoptic gospels, creating faith in this way is considered vulgar.

Below is a smattering of alleged miracles from both the New Testament and the Old. Viewed with a modern eye, most of the claims are beyond ridiculous. But whatever portion might possibly belong both to the historical and the paranormal, the question arises, do we really want to continue creating a world in which we are content to remain bedazzled by those committed to using these stories to control us?

The Bible "miraculously" gives three contradictory accounts on the death of King Saul. In the first, Saul kills himself (1 Samuel 31:4); in the second, Saul is killed by an Amalekite (2 Samuel 1:10); and finally, a Philistine kills him (2 Samuel 21:12). But devils in the details aside, there's no question that it's hard to keep a good man down!

The Bible tells us that Melchizedek had no parents (Genesis 2:7). The great thing about this is, by not having to purchase Mother's Day and Father's Day cards and gifts, this biblical hero always had extra beer money.

Impressive as it is on the scale of miracles that Melchizedek had no parents and therefore no genealogy (Hebrews 7:3), Jesus Christ outdoes him big time, having no less than two paternal grandfathers. In Matthew 1:16, we learn that one of the guy's names was Jacob, the other, Heli, (Luke 3:23).

In an under reported miracle, Moses (the alleged author of all five books of the Pentateuch) seems to recount the details of his own funeral (Deuteronomy 34: 5-6). This would seem to indicate that, whether or not the dead can dance, they certainly can narrate.

When Moses strikes his staff twice on a rock at Meribah, he gets plenty of drinking water for the faithful and their animals (Number

20:7-11). If this stunt hadn't worked, people might have said Moses was off his rocker.

Never mind the cliché that says you can't get blood out of stone. Moses at least got water out of a rock at Rephidim (Exodus 17:5-7) and the Israelites no doubt agreed, it made for much better tasting and drinking.

In Exodus 14:21, Moses parts the Red Sea. Since this Jewish patriarch tended to be something of a jerk, the parting was something less than sweet sorrow and likely even lacked a low budget going away party.

Yahweh commands Moses to sprinkle some dirt towards the sky as a means of making boils break out on people (and animals) throughout the land of Egypt (Exodus 9:10). Consequently, finding the right make-up for prom night proved a bitch.

Upon God's command, Moses stretches his hand over the hand of Egypt and causes a gigantic swarm of locusts to arise (Exodus 12:19). The locusts subsequently destroy Egyptian agriculture, eating everyone out of house and home until, upon Pharaoh's repentance, they are blown into the Red Sea to the tune of Dylan's "Don't Think Twice, It's All Right."

The biblical God commands Moses to stretch his hand towards the sky as a magical way of making it dark, and consequently this darkness falls upon Egypt for three days (Exodus 10:21-22). Most Egyptians end up agreeing that lots of extra sex and additional sleep represented a positive outcome, and they, therefore, dreaded the return of the light.

Moses heads off the collective murmurs against him by his people by turning bitter drinking water sweet. He does this by throwing a tree into the water, then uses the miracle as leverage in creating a new statute and ordinance. (Exodus 15:23-25).

The biblical God commands Aaron to stretch out his sword and strike the earth with it, so that the land might become full of lice,

63

covering humans and animals alike (Exodus 8:16). The lice treatment companies and their shareholders were of course delighted, but became somewhat annoyed when the Pharaoh's magicians were unable to duplicate the miracle.

The Bible tells us that Jesus Christ's holy predecessors Enoch and Elijah both ascended into heaven, Elijah even getting to ride up in a two-wheel drive chariot. It can therefore be argued that Jesus' claim of no one having ascended into heaven prior to him (John 3:13) is not only bogus, but couldn't possibly have been made by the Lord with a straight face.

If Jesus Christ fed 5,000 men plus the uncounted women and children with five loaves of bread and two fishes (Matthew 14:13-21), the argument could be made that he missed his calling. Perhaps he should have gone into the restaurant business.

On another occasion, Jesus Christ apparently feeds 4,000 folks from seven loaves of bread and a few fish. The closest Old Testament competitor to the Lord is Elisha who disappointingly is only able to feed 100 men with twenty loaves and a little newly ripened grain from his knapsack.

Jesus Christ's alchemically transmuting water into wine at the marriage feast at Cana was no small feat (John 2:1-11). Even more impressive would have been the Lord's manifesting Long Island Iced Tea.

Whether Jesus Christ is correct in alleging that those who believe in him will be able to pick up snakes and live to tell the tale ((Mark 16:18), the additional claim that these believers will be able to drink deadly things and not die is definitely true. Christians have been drinking Coca-Cola since 1886 and no one has immediately expired from it, the sugar poison and other toxins patiently taking their time to work their mischief.

Apparently unconcerned about hygiene and all-things-sanitary, Jesus Christ uses his own spit to heal a man who had been blind since birth (John 9:6). Had the Lord failed in His endeavor, the man would likely have reached out and tried to choke Him.

At Isaiah the Prophet's request, and no doubt to his delight, the biblical God causes a shadow to move ten steps back on a sundial (2 Kings 20:11). As if things weren't problematic enough already for Peter Pan.

By the power of under reported miracles, Jesus Christ and his companions are said to have arrived in two cities that didn't exist at the time, Sychar (John 4:5) and Bethabara (John 1:28). This only goes to show that, as the Bible claims, with God all things are very much possible.

According to the Bible, seizures are caused by demons, and this is especially true regarding the kind that cause people to fall into fire and water. We learn about this sort of thing in Matthew 17:18 in which Jesus Christ delivers a boy possessed by a seizure demon.

One particular fellow in the Bible finds himself tongue-tied on account of apparently being possessed by an introverted demon who favored silence over chatter. Once Jesus Christ drives the demon out, the guy starts blabbing again, everyone agreeing in amazement they had never seen anything like this before (Matthew 9:32,33).

An unclean spirit possessing one particular guy feels threatened and rightly so, since the Lord promptly exorcises it (Mark 1:23-28). The Bible is mum on whether the spirit was allowed to return after a shower.

An iron ax head falls into some water and upon the command from a man of God, it not only floats, but swims (2 Kings 6:5-6). The U.S. Olympic swimming team senses a great opportunity and issues iron bathing suits to all team members.

Jesus Christ might well have slept through a furious storm while riding in a boat on a lake except that His disciples, fearful that the boat was about to sink wake Him up. Calling these disciples faithless, the Lord commands both the wind and waves to chill and both do (Matthew 8:23-26). This secures the Lord's reputation for all time and eternity as a bastion of weather modification skill.

.

Chapter Nine: 'SMALL' ISSUES WITH THE BIBLE AT LARGE

"What people believe is truly unbelievable."
-- Swami Beyondananda

Assuming you aren't among the rare, tortured souls who have read in full at least one of the 50+ English translations of the Bible, a great many random verses tends to strike the reader as extremely odd! This may especially be the case if, religious indoctrination (brainwashing) aside, you cannot in good conscience justify and endorse monstrosities like cannibalism, violence-laced racism, or divinely decreed amputation, not to mention blatant sexism and even genocide.

Never mind that the Bible by its own arrogant admission claims to be synonymous with Divine Reality, posing as it does, as the inerrant Word of God. Quite frankly, this is a joke or would be except that the mass hypnotic state the claim induces in its followers is really no laughing matter.

Let's face it: in spite of all its bravado, posing, and posturing, our endangered species remains prone to the degradation of woefully sloppy thinking. Did a donkey really speak fluent Hebrew (Numbers 22:28)? How about the silver- tongued serpent living rent free in Eden (Genesis 3:1)? Did an iron bar really float in water (2 Kings 6:6)? Did Moses achieve the ultimate water trick and successfully part the Red Sea (Exodus 14:21)?

Disturbing as it is, religionists, including modern era Christians, somehow are okay with allowing the heavy lifting portions of biblical interpretation to be done by the so called experts, mostly the well fed, well paid clergy. Innate to this devil's bargain, the entrusted priest or minister cherry picks verses, conveniently circumventing problematic ones that defy logic, on the one hand, or even sanely-sound ethics, on the other. The flock is told to relegate all of the weirdness to the realm of mystery. The promised consolation prize is knowing that God will eventually reveal the conciliatory truth to you on the wings of earnest prayer. Or maybe on the other side of the veil when you die and fly up to heaven.

But heaven can definitely wait and if we want to co-create a world paradigm worth having and sustaining (certainly one which more scrupulously separates the values of Church and State), we are going to have to do better than looking to religious anachronisms like the Bible as sources of truth and guidance.

1 Peter 4:3 says that in the past, Christians were influenced by the will of the Gentiles, frankly walking in lasciviousness, lust, excess of wine, reveling, banqueting, and abominable idolatry. But this doesn't mean there weren't bad times, too.

We read in Acts 2:3 that the Holy Spirit fell upon those saints gathered for Pentecost. Fortunately, there were no reported injuries.

In Ezra 9:3 we find the prophet pulling out his hair and beard upon learning that the Jews had intermarried with other races. It was clearly a whole new look for him, although the Holy Bible doesn't say whether or not going hairless generally made him hotter to women.

Even the most finely bred men and women are going to cannibalize their children in one particularly difficult famine, even as they refuse to share the meat with their spouses or family members (Deuteronomy 28:53-57). Those who are deprived likely go vegan, saving money in the process.

Exodus 22:18 says that one should not suffer a female magician or sorceress to live. This no doubt pleased the multitude of true believers just dying to kill them.

Apparently the wicked are estranged as early as their experience in the womb, going astray and speaking lies as soon as they are born (Psalms 58:3). Therefore, beware precocious, silver-tongued devils in diapers lest you be woefully deceived.

Proverbs 11:29 brings us a lot to digest inasmuch as we are told that people who bring trouble on their families "inherit the wind." Unfortunately, those of us around the given culprit tend to inherit the consequences of the wind, most distressingly perhaps, when riding in crowded cars and buses affording no merciful escape.

The book of Ruth is used in the Jewish faith to instruct daughters-in-law on how to submit to mothers-in-law. This scripture thus became the original inspiration for the prescribed use of Prozac and Xanax among young women sporting the biblical brand.

Apparently everyone who sins comes from the devil (John 3:8). Since, according to Christian doctrine we are all sinners, straightening out this mess has hellishly given our species one devil of a time.

Peter, James and John not only fell asleep for much of the Transfiguration experience (Luke 9:32), but in the Garden of Gethsemane as well (Luke 22:40). The Spirit may or may not have been willing, but the flesh was weak or the wine spirits and weed, way too strong.

Tired of high electric or gas bills associated with cooking and baking? Why not follow scripture and use human poop for your stove's fuel (Ezekiel 4:12)?

Yahweh is reportedly the "perfect gift-giving Father of Lights in whom there is no shadow or variance" (James 1:17). Shadow or variance aside, however, He apparently does create evil (Isaiah 45:7), lots of it.

The Bible says that it's appointed to man to die once (Hebrews 9:27). But if you add in the possibility of the Second Death (Revelation 21:8), it becomes once or twice, or if the doctrine of reincarnation is true, you can probably stop counting.

If you keep the whole law, but mess up on even one point, you are guilty of *every type of sin* (James 2:10). It can therefore be stated that, by lying, Pinocchio is clearly guilty of murder and adultery, not to mention blasphemously taking the Lord's name in vain.

Is money really the root of all evil (1 Timothy 6:10)? Certainly not for the hedonistic writer of Ecclesiastes who, over optimistically, claims that money answers everything (Ecclesiastes 10:19).

Near-irrefutable proof that Moses and the Israelites never stopped to ask for directions is evidenced by the biblical admission that they wandered in the tiny Sinai Desert for forty years (Numbers 32:13). Is it any wonder Jesus Christ acknowledges having been sent only unto the lost tribes of Israel?

Since King Solomon had in the neighborhood of 700 wives and 300 concubines (First Kings 11:3), it's probably safe to assume that the palace was pretty crowded. And, quite frankly, the cost of Valentine's Day and birthday gifts alone would explain the inordinately high tax rate in the kingdom.

On the one hand, the Father doesn't judge anyone, all judgment having been committed to the Son and, on the other hand, the Son by his own admission, doesn't judge anyone (John 8:15, 12:47).

This leaves the task of judgment to the Comforter Spirit, which, in a word, is rather discomforting.

The precursor of The Thing depicted in The Addams Family makes its debut in Daniel 5:5-6. There we find a hand writing in plaster, offering us the prophetic writing on the wall.

The Bible informs us that corn will make the young men cheerful, and new wine, the maids (Zechariah 9:17). There's little question the maids got the better part of the deal, for a change.

Chapter Ten: THE "INERRANT" WORD OF GOD: GREATEST HITS

"If you think we are not here to make mistakes, you are mistaken."
-- Swami Beyondananda

The perversely-quaint notion that the Bible is the inerrant (yup, error-free!) Word of God brought directly to us from on High is, quite frankly, way beyond ridiculous. The renowned researcher and scholar C. Dennis McKinsey attempted to illustrate this in his epic book, The Encyclopedia of Biblical Errancy. McKinsey categorizes all of the hundreds of errors made in the Bible. Unfortunately for McKinsey and those of us who share his vision of an anachronism-free world, sales of his book are stuck in the mere tens of thousands, compared to the Bible which is at five billion and rising. Of course one's purchasing a Bible is much more common than one actually reading it. And there's no question that a certain percentage of Bibles largely end up serving as a place for dust mite villages.

The fact remains, however, the Bible is humanity's #1 best seller. The Bible's supreme popularity, relative to those literary offerings put out by its competitors and detractors, simply amazes or rather, startles. Why? Because the "Good Book" isn't really quite as good as it is advertised to be, the hundreds

of errors being only part of the problem. Ethics is lacking in the extreme. So is logic. Consider, for example, the absurdity of the early Church Father Tertullian claiming that the reason the Resurrection must be true is because it's absurd! Yowza!

Jesus Christ wants you to know that Adam and Eve really did exist, and not just in the imagination of the Genesis author (Matthew 19:4). And since Adam had no biological parents and Eve had no mother, it became imperative for our original parents to read Dr. Spock's voluminous books on child rearing.

The biblical God simultaneously creates man in his own image, male and female (Genesis 1:27). Confusingly, though, He later creates Eve out of Adam's rib (2:21-23), no doubt causing our original Mother to say, "What the hell's going on here; I thought I already existed!?"

Even though the biblical God tells Adam that he'll die if he eats the forbidden fruit (Genesis 2:17), Adam lives to the overripe old age of 930 (Genesis 5:5). Everyone was likely happy to see Adam go, the cost of his geriatric medications alone having become prohibitive.

Isaiah 44:14 tells us about someone's planting an ash tree in western Asia, which the rain nourished. Since ash trees don't currently grow in that area and never have, the passage makes about as much sense as would claiming that a palm tree was successfully planted and subsequently fructified in Antarctica.

Isaiah 24:20 tells us that our troubled earth, weighted down by sin (and presumably the multitudes who eat too much pasta) will pass away with transgressions. You can therefore kiss goodbye the overly optimistic Bible verses claiming that earth is established forever! (Psalm 104:5, Psalm 78:69, Ecclesiastes 1:4).

In 2 Kings 15:19, we learn that an Assyrian king named Pul "came against the land". Since Assyria never had a king named Pul, we can speculate on the possibility that the biblical author is pulling a fast one here.

Did King Solomon have 40,000 stalls for his royal horses (1st Kings 4:26) or just 4,000, as indicated in 2nd Chronicles 9:25? This question is perhaps less important to lay persons and clergy than to those assigned to clean the stalls.

How could a temple measuring a mere 96' x 32' x 48' (1 Kings 6:2) take seven years to build (1 Kings 7:38), especially since King Solomon had hired for the project some 70,000 carriers and 80,000 stone cutters (including 33,000 supervisors)? The likely answer is, a superbly-agreeable union contract and some really great weed.

2 Samuel 24:9 tells us that, in one given battle, 800,000 men drew the sword, but 1 Chronicles 21:5 says the number was actually 1,100,000. Given this biblical discrepancy of 300,000, is it possible the sword was sketched or painted rather than drawn?

Ahaziah begins to rule his father's kingdom at age twenty-two (2 Kings 8:26). Miraculously, however, he also begins ruling at age forty-two (2 Chronicles 22:2), thus making him twenty years his father's senior and someone no longer needing to beg for an allowance.

If Bethlehem is in Galilee rather than Judea, as confidently stated in scripture (John 7:41-42), then Houston, TX is a suburb of Wichita, KS, Moscow is the capitol of Indonesia, and you've accepted Poseidon as your Personal Lord and Savior.

We learn from John 4:5 that Jesus Christ came to a city of Samaria named Sychar. Except that there wasn't any city in Samaria named Sychar at the time, the passage stands as a grand testimonial to the unquestionable truth of biblical inerrancy.

Jesus Christ departs from Galilee, supposedly leaving the town of Nazareth and dwelling in Capernaum (Matthew 4:12,13). Since Nazareth is a suburb of Capernaum and is also in Galilee, the Bible seems to have departed from the geographical truth here, as in so many other places.

John 12:21 identifies Bethsaida as being in Galilee, although it's actually in another district, Gaulonitis. Since the name of both places begin with the letter "g", it can be argued that the Bible is at least partially correct.

According to Acts 1:12, the hill called the Mount of Olives was a Sabbath day's journey walk from the city. But since this hill was actually right outside the Jerusalem wall nearest the Temple, we can assume that whoever wrote this passage was using a walker or quad cane, or perhaps moving himself along in a pre-electric wheel chair.

Jesus Christ claims that Jonah spent time inside of a whale (Matthew 12:40) which is of course a mammal, whereas Jonah 1:17 says it was inside a fish. Theologians have had a whale of a time trying to reconcile that which is explicitly, irrefutably fishy.

Did Satan first take Jesus Christ up onto the pinnacle of the Temple, then up a high mountain (Matthew 4:5-8) or up the mountain, then onto the Temple pinnacle (Luke 4:5-9)? And if there is an explanation which avoids contradiction, could it be that Jesus and the Devil made two separate trips, being careful not to offend posterity's Christian fundamentalists?

Chapter Eleven: THE SUB-SUPREME ACCURACY OF BIBLICAL PROPHECY

"I never make predictions. That way I'm able to keep my non-prophet status."
--Swami Beyondananda

The author of Old Testament Deuteronomy tells his readers not to be afraid of a presumptuous prophet (18:22). In other words, if what a prophet says doesn't come to pass, don't take the guy's prophecy or the guy himself too seriously. In fact, the Bible weirdly claims that you must not merely chastise him verbally in the way, for example, Mr. Geppetto does with Pinocchio, but rather put the poor bastard to death (Deuteronomy 13:5). It's tough stuff, talk about substantial job stress! Being an air traffic controller would be a cakewalk compared to serving as a prophet in ancient Israel. It had to get old!

Hyrum Smith, brother of Mormon founder Joseph Smith, apparently argued the point that a prophet hardly needs to score anywhere close to 100% with prophetic accuracy in order to remain viable. This seems reasonable enough, given that life is an ever changing kaleidoscope of shifting information, and there are even places where prophecies are changed or reversed by the Lord Himself, surprise, surprise!

For example, the sinful city of Nineveh had been prophetically scheduled to be destroyed by Yahweh after forty days. The Lord did change His mind and repented of the prophesied annihilation. The people of the city no doubt came out in mass to give Him a collective thumbs-up, not middle finger, and maybe even a well-deserved standing ovation.

There are also times where God makes good on His omnipresent threats, and in Genesis 6:6, we find Him getting pissed off for even creating humans; and, in fact, in the same chapter He shockingly commits near-universal genocide via the Flood. Also startling is the series of fifteen Old Testament passages where He complains that He's just about to do something He might later regret, His self- control and emotional IQ perhaps being a bit lower than the faithful faithfully suppose.

However much any of us may appreciate prophets with high batting averages, even as all ultimately fall short of the mathematical glory of 100%, the biblical God feels differently, and the Bible tells us so. For Yahweh, the utterance of a true prophecy testified to the given prophet's authenticity; false prophecy indicated that the prophet was not a legitimate bearer of the Lord's brand and was merely operating out of His own imagination or that of seducing spirits. In essence, it was a rigged system, and the Lord had the major home court advantage of cynically-predetermined credibility. The onus of prophetic proof was always on the prophet, not the biblical God, regardless of prophetic outcome. This system effectively immunized Yahweh from having to have His omniscience tested.

At the end of the ominous day, the Bible is a scripture that is chock-full of false prophecies which ironically are falsely listed as true. That Christianity and its angry single parent, Judaism, haven't been called out on this in any significant way is unconscionable. Let's shed, or better yet shine, some well-deserved light now on this bizarre phenomenon.

No less than nine passages in the Old Testament say that the Messiah's arrival will usher in a time of sinlessness, and at least fourteen more verses claim the arrival will result in bringing a one world religion. As you can see simply by looking around you, sinlessness lies in ruins and there are only around 35000 Christian denominations today, praise the Risen Lord.

It matters little outside the realm of false prophecy that Jesus Christ declared that some standing with Him wouldn't taste death until they saw the Son of Man coming in his kingdom (Matthew 16:28). The Son was of course a no-show and everyone standing with the Lord apparently did taste death, even as it apparently tasted them.

Prophetically, there were supposed to be five Egyptian cities that ended up speaking the language of Canaan (Isaiah 19:18). This language is now extinct, the prophecy having remained unfulfilled, although pet owners in this nation, especially dog whisperers, do sometimes speak the language of canine.

The biblical God proves He's all wet in claiming that the Nile River would dry up (Ezekiel 30:12) and all its fish thus disappear (Zechariah 10:11). Since this huge waterway is still flowing strong and its fish still swimming, it's the case that these "prophetic" passages, like so many others, have hung prophecy-minded Biblicists out to dry, and thus became dehydrated.

The biblical God was supposed to have utterly destroyed Egypt and killed everyone living there (Jeremiah 42:17), but His plan apparently went a little awry. The current population of Egypt is now close to 100 million and growing.

The biblical God assures us that Egypt would be conquered by Nebuchadnezzar (Ezekiel 29:15-21). Whether or not the king and his army ever actually campaigned there, conquest of this nation was never successfully achieved and therefore the Lord's assurance is somewhat less than reassuring.

According to Ezekiel 27:36, the city of Tyre was to have come to a horrible end, ceasing to exist forevermore. With a robust population today of roughly 174,000, the best tourist attraction of this ancient Lebanese city is apparently the Al-Bass archaeological site. If you go there, don't forget your sunscreen, climate change being enough to worry about.

Hazor was the name of four biblical places, although none of these seem to have been inhabited by dragons, as the Bible claims (Jeremiah 49:33). In fact, there weren't even any two-legged dragons called wyverines, which had to be something of a disappointment to J.R.R. Tolkien and his hobbit friends living in the shire section of one of the four Hazors.

Isaiah 17:1-2 prophesies that Damascus would cease to be a city. Despite the best efforts of all the competing foreign and domestic powers trying to make this happen, the city is still standing, but could probably benefit from a well-deserved rest, maybe one featuring free massages for all and group hug circles for the willing.

If Isaiah 9:6 is prophetically alluding to Jesus Christ, then the Son of Man would appear to have something of an identity crisis, apparently being both the Prince of Peace and the Everlasting Father (King of Kings). Now this would no doubt be a really tough row to hoe, especially given the question, "Who is supposed to give whom presents on Christmas or the eight days of Hanukkah?"

If the voice of Psalm 69:21-28 really were that of Jesus Christ, then it could be argued that the Prince of Peace seems to be a bit cranky on certain days. If you read further, the referenced psalmist goes on to ask the biblical God to blind his enemies, destroy their habitation, and subject them to various other causes of pain including blotting out their names from the Book of Life.

Jesus Christ, a self-made God-Man, boasts to his enemies that, if they kill him, He'll engineer His return from the dead in just three days (John 2:19). Never mind that Acts 2:24 and Acts 13:30 both say that God would be the one doing the resurrecting.

In Luke 4:17-21, Jesus Christ creatively (and destructively) spices up Isaiah 61:1-2 by blatantly misquoting it. There is, in fact, absolutely nothing mentioned in the Prophet's quote about restoring eye sight to the blind, whether through applying spittle or, more hygienically, supplying the people in question with eyeglasses or contact lenses.

While Jesus Christ boldly declares in Matthew 10:7 that the kingdom is at hand, the question is, whose hand? Despite the clarion call for patient faith, the Lord definitely has not drawn nigh as scheduled (James 5:8) and he who was supposed to come (Hebrews 10:37) still hasn't and likely won't, the faithful apparently being stuck in a futile exercise of waiting for Godot.

Jeremiah 34:4-5 confidently prophesied that King Zedekiah would experience a peaceful death. But after the king of Babylon kills Zedekiah's sons right in front of him and then proceeds to poke out both of the King's eyes, Zedekiah is thrown into a stinking dungeon where he rots away and finally perishes, not quite in peace, as prophesied.

Jesus Christ's confident claim that Moses prophetically wrote about Him (John 5:46) is off-the-proverbial wall. As Thomas Paine, author of *The Age of Reason* proves beyond the shadow of a doubt or Doubting Thomas, there's not a single word written in the Old Testament Bible about Jesus Christ, a slew of prophetic attributions notwithstanding.

Jesus Christ tells His skeptical fellow Jews that if they believed in Moses, they'd believe in Him because Moses testified of Him (John 5:46). Now, if the minority opinion among religious historians is true, and neither Moses nor Jesus actually existed, we are left with the peculiar phenomenon of one fiction confidently testifying of another, and non-fictionally.

Jesus Christ confidently proclaims John the Baptist to be the renewed Elijah (Matthew 11:14). The fly in the ointment, a gigantic one the size of a woolly mammoth, is that John himself argues the case for mistaken identity, saying he definitely is not the renewed Elijah (John 1:21).

Apparently all you have to do is ask the biblical God for something in Jesus Christ's name and it will be expeditiously fulfilled (John 14:13,14.)? Ya, right!

Based upon an interesting interpretation of Zechariah 9:9, one featuring a Jesus Christ retrofitted to deviously support prophetic claim, the Matthew author has Jesus Christ not just riding into Jerusalem on a donkey (Mark 11:1-10, Luke 19:28-40), but rather, straddling a colt and a donkey (Matthew 21:1-7). This is one occasion among many in which the gospel writer and former tax collector clearly makes an ass of himself.

Read in context, the individual mentioned in Isaiah 53:4 is not someone who heals lepers, but is himself a leper! Christian apologists claiming that the passage prophetically speaks of Jesus Christ clearly are stuck in a diseased perspective that twists and turns the truth 180 degrees.

Matthew 27:9,10 alludes to a prophecy by someone he calls Jeremy the Prophet (see Jeremiah 32:6-9) which, unfortunately, doesn't seem to exist anywhere in the Book of Jeremiah, neither the names Jack, Jill, Jim, or Jerry. The passage itself is relatively unimportant, which is good, even if Matthew's apparent mental fog isn't.

In Hebrews 1:5, the Pauline author misidentified as the Apostle Paul quotes 2 Samuel 7:14 as prophetic proof of Jesus Christ, but conveniently cuts short the passage. If he hadn't done so, scripture would have clearly shown the author was talking about King Solomon, not Christianity's future Lord.

It's high time Christian apologists got high and apologized for claiming that Psalm 41:1 is prophetically speaking of Jesus Christ. The person in question identifies himself not as someone who is even remotely sinless, but rather as a sinner in need of healing.

Isaiah 7:15 speaks of a guy (supposedly Jesus Christ) who will eat butter and honey so that he may choose the good and refuse the evil. Oddly enough, there's no pictures or portraits showing the Lord as overweight or with rotten teeth.

Wishful thinking aside on the part of Christian prophecy buffs, Psalm 41:9 isn't fulfilling scripture by speaking of Judas Iscariot's betrayal of Jesus Christ (Acts 1:16). King David, the author of the given Psalm, was clearly betrayed by his own friend, not someone from the future, although there's still a lot of this going around.

Prophetically speaking, no uncircumcised person was ever again to have entered the city of Jerusalem (Isaiah 52:1). Since cutting an infant (or person of any age) is now considered cruel by many, let's be grateful that the uncircumcised population of the holy city is still alive and well.

Since the Israelites ended up being in Babylonian captivity for forty-eight, not seventy, years we can safely say that 2 Chronicles 36:20 -21 is nothing remotely resembling the fulfillment of Jeremiah 25:11. It is, however, the crystal clear fulfillment of really bad math.

After identifying himself as the harbinger of the Gospel of Jesus Christ, Son of God (Mark 1:1), the Mark author immediately tries to quote a passage from the prophet Isaiah. This turns out to be somewhat problematic, but only in the sense that what he quotes doesn't actually exist (Mark 1:2).

Is Jesus Christ the scepter that would never depart from Judah (Genesis 49:10)? The answer is, only if you disregard 2 Kings 25:8 which, unfortunately, informs us that the scepter frankly did depart from Judah, and some 588 years before Jesus Christ was allegedly born.

The Bible prophetically foretells that lions will finally eat straw (Isaiah 65:17). So far, so bad for those poor creatures still being preyed upon by the king of the jungle, this predator only eating straw during participation in weight loss programs.

The silliness of John 19:37 notwithstanding, Zechariah 12:10 is no more about Jesus Christ crucified than it might be about a guy choosing to attract more intentional body piercings. Read in context, Zechariah, Chapter 12 concerns itself, not with messianic prophecy, but rather, a future military invasion.

Chapter Twelve: THE EVER-SEXY BIBLE, NOT!

"I was celibate for fourteen years, but when I turned
fifteen, I said 'Enough of that!' "
-- Swami Beyondananda

If you were to come to the Bible based on the idea that this
scripture is in any way sexy, you'd be sadly mistaken. With the
exception of parts of The Song of Solomon, the Bible lacks sex
appeal in the extreme, being full of all sorts of problems that
would trouble any self-respecting sex therapist or patient.

Sex is certainly an interesting topic. Fortunately, sex has cum a
long way since the biblical days of yore, which seem to have felt
so much more uptight. For example, excepting the special
privileges of so-called royalty, patriarchs, and a few other
select affiliates from the world of muckety mucks, non-
monogamous sexuality wasn't exactly applauded, the same
being the case with free expression of sexual orientation.

Condemnation of ostensibly unorthodox sexuality does
continue having deep roots within certain segments of the
religious population, a significant segment of Christian,
Muslim, and Mormon church/mosque/temple goers come
immediately to mind. Within the confines of Latter Day Saint
belief, for example, young people are fervently warned to avoid

like a soul plague committing the "deadly" sin of masturbation, not least because all of the masturbators' ancestors would be watching from above in deep condemnation. The message? Simply that if you want to be invited to family gatherings in the afterlife bliss of the Celestial Kingdom, don't risk your ticket to otherworldly paradise by jerking off or playing with a vibrator in the earthly, earthy here and now.

Sex is a phenomenon of enormous power, one which our species has yet to figure out, even if our horny primate cousins the bonobos largely have. In any case, be rest or restless assured: there is nothing in the Bible that moves us in the direction of healthy sexual freedom. There is, however, quite a lot that aims to move us in the opposite direction: that of repression, neurosis, and self-torment. All I can say is - buyer be aware, buyer beware.

If you lived in Old Testament times and got caught having sex with your neighbor's wife, you were to be put to death (Leviticus 20:10). If you committed the misdeed on the Sabbath, you'd likely have to be put to death twice.

God's humble servant Onan is slain by Yahweh for opting to spank the monkey and spill his seed on the ground rather than cum inside his brother's wife (Genesis 38:9-10). In biblical times "getting caught with your pants down" wasn't just embarrassing. It was sometimes fatal.

The Lord calls out a group of horny Israelite males who like lusty stallions busy themselves, neighing for their neighbors' wives (Jeremiah 5:8). Given that the mares were doing a little neighing of their own, there thus began the popular phenomenon called swinging.

The Lord plans to lift gals' skirts up to their faces in order to shame them (Nahum 3:5). The delayed reaction came in the form of the

Me Too Movement, the first creepy male offender being the Ancient of Days.

Yahweh apparently liked to flirt with the head of the daughters of Zion and sometimes to go beyond mere flirting, discovering her secret parts (Isaiah 3:17). But since He originally created her, it really couldn't have been much of a discovery.

Jesus Christ is going to throw Queen Jezebel into a bed along with those who commit adultery with her (Revelation 2:22). Hopefully these legion souls won't break the springs.

Being old enough for love, Jerusalem is praised by the biblical God for her pretty hair and well-formed breasts (Ezekiel 16:7-8). There's no mention of the city daring to reply: "Stop being so shallow, Lord."

During a divinely-ordained slaughter of the Midianites, the Israelites on Moses' command spare 32000 virgins as booty for his lieutenants (Numbers 31:18). Even Yahweh Himself receives a share of the booty, 32 virgins in all, praise the Lord (Numbers 31:41)!

Never mind that the Bible wants to execute judgment on you, and in fact, execute you in the event you are gay (Leviticus 18:22). Solemnity certainly sucks, and in all the wrong places.

If you are gay or fall into a few other categories, you won't inherit the Kingdom of God (1 Corinthians 6:9,10). You might, however, be eligible for a round of drinks in the Christian version of hell with King David who apparently told his friend Jonathan that he was better in bed than any women (2 Samuel 1:26).

It is apparently good for a man not to touch a woman (1 Corinthians 7:1). But rather than face the bleak option of celibacy, some straight men no doubt began touching other men, hoping to get around Paul's injunction.

Regarding the coming Rapture, Jesus Christ shares with us: "I tell you, in that night there shall be two men in one bed; the one shall be taken and the other shall be left." (Luke 17:34-35) The Rapture aside, the two men in bed won't likely take kindly to this sort of unnecessary interruption.

2 Kings 24:6 informs us that Jehoiakim, the ruler of Judah, slept with his fathers. Although at first glance this may strike one as rather kinky, as in the incestuous taboo sense demonstrated by Ham (Genesis 9:22), it's not quite what it seems, "sleeping" being a mere euphemism for death.

A bishop in the early Church was allowed only one wife (1 Timothy 3:2) and the same was true for deacons (1 Timothy 3:12). You can take it to the bank that there wasn't a bishop or deacon anywhere in earshot of the Beach Boys' hit single, "Two Girls for Every Boy."

Leviticus 20:14 says that if a man marries a woman and the woman's mom, all three are to be burnt alive. This gives hot sex a whole new meaning.

In Matthew 25:1-11 only five out of ten virgins remember to fill their lamps with oil and so when the polygamous bridegroom shows up unexpectedly one night, only half of the women are available to bed him. It was likely a pretty good night for the guy nonetheless.

God apparently created humans with an innate need and desire for the close (sexual) bond that marriage provides (Proverbs 18:22). This well explains why divorce is now a thing of the past.

In Ezekiel 23:22, the biblical God tells his vexed servant Oholibah that He will raise this guy's lovers up against him from every direction -- including from those very nations from which he had turned away in disgust. And you thought monogamy was challenging?

Loving your neighbor is subject to certain minor limitations in the Bible. For example, if you enjoy sexual intercourse with her or him, the party will soon be over, but only in the sense you'll both be promptly executed (Leviticus 20:10).

The God of the Bible seems to have given certain women up to vile sexual affections (Romans 1:26), meaning lesbian or bisexual partying. But with orgasmic potential suddenly skyrocketing for these sinners, life became deliciously wetter and wilder, and significantly less encumbered by the sickly restrictions innate in patriarchal tyranny.

The widow who is all about pleasure, including sexual pleasure, is apparently dead even while she lives (1 Timothy 5:6). This issue notwithstanding, these living-dead losers are apparently capable of throwing some really great parties.

The Bible isn't sheepish about informing us that capital punishment is the price for sleeping with an animal (Leviticus 20:15-16). Beware, all you college age women who are even thinking about dating frat boys.

The Bible offers hope in more ways than meet the naked eye. For example, having apparently found an excellent male enhancement supplement, whether or not FDA approved, the apostle Paul tells those Christian men who are apparently not very well endowed: "Be ye also enlarged" (2 Corinthians 6:13).

The Bible is intensely critical of the human body's natural propensity to orgasm, demanding that the faithful not make provisions for the flesh to fulfill its lusts (Romans 13:14). You can therefore go on faith that this wasn't good news for the Empire's various sex shops or vibrator manufacturing outlets.

According to Romans 8:6, to be carnally-minded is death itself. Be that as it may, the argument can be made in favor of hot sex since sexual repression is something worse, namely, death-warmed-over.

We learn from Psalm 38:5-7 that King David suffered from a stinking, festering STD. The Bible is silent on how many lovers "God's Anointed" may have infected, no doubt writing these victims off as collateral damage.

The Apostle Paul's shameless admitting that he is in bonds (Ephesians 6:20) is frankly over the top. The apostle's proclivity for B & D is no one's business but his own and that of his chosen playmates.

If you are born of God you cannot commit sin and your seed will remain in you (1 John 5:18). Be that as it volitionally may, if you happen to have even one wet dream and the Lord finds out, you're likely screwed.

Paul wants every Christian husband and wife to know that they have power over each other's bodies, but not their own, masturbation apparently being a terribly grave sin (1 Corinthians 7:4). Paul's interpretation of the "hands off" approach has been a bitch for some believers.

Wives beware, if you interfere in a brawl between your husband and another guy, and the intervention specifically involves your grabbing your hubby's adversary by the balls, the Lord decrees that the offending hand, namely yours, be cut off (Deuteronomy 25:11-12). If this occurs, guys, your spouse will have one great excuse for not giving you future hand jobs on demand.

A Christian husband and wife are to render one another due conjugal benevolence (1 Corinthians 7:3). So, if you need a big favor, but have been afraid to ask, maybe wait until after your spouse orgasms.

You had better fast and pray so that Satan doesn't tempt with incontinence (1 Corinthians 7:5). Peeing your pants while at the mall or on a date could be very embarrassing indeed.

When the priests come to arrest Jesus Christ in the Garden of Gethsemane, at least one young male follower of the Lord drops his drawers or linen cloth and flees bare-assed naked into the night (Mark 14:51-52). Only Dr. Morton Smith and a small minority of religious historians have dared suggest that something like an all-male hot tub party had been in progress prior to the interruption.

Among other things, the Apostle Paul wants to make known to you his affairs (Ephesians 6:20). Since Paul boasts about being celibate, his having even a single affair would be quite disturbing.

If a betrothed virgin is raped in the city, but doesn't cry out loud enough, she is to be stoned to death (Deuteronomy 22:23-24). All women lacking a great pair of lungs are therefore advised to buy a megaphone or quickly relocate to the country.

Ten of King David's concubines are raped by David's son Absalom. All the women are punished by the king for permitting the rape, being condemned to perpetual maid service coupled with strict celibacy (2 Samuel 15:16).

Samson's mom Manoah testifies that a man of God came inside her without revealing his name and without her asking him any questions (Judges 13:6). We can only pray God told him to use a rubber.

It goes unmentioned whether or not the Apostle Paul in a rage grabbed someone by the balls. It was, however, Paul's expressed desire that the surgical knife of circumcision slip and cut off the penises of certain among his rivals-for-power and dominance (Galatians 5:12).

The two daughters of the biblical patriarch Lot hang out in a cave with their dad for a while and after getting him drunk, also succeed in having him impregnate them. Lot denies knowledge of both events (Genesis 33:36), even as he would have likely had trouble explaining how, the alcohol level notwithstanding, he apparently had no trouble getting it up.

A man should not sleep with his mother or discover his father's skirts (Judges 22:30). Oedipal concerns aside for the moment, the son is well advised to stay the hell out of his cross-dressing father's wardrobe.

The biblical God is quite upset that His daughter Jerusalem apparently has sex with strangers, paying them to come into her from every side (Ezekiel 16:33). Ancient sexologists were no doubt bewildered, not least because even if this holy city had been in the sandwich position, there would only have been possible entry from two sides.

Chapter Thirteen: NON-HUMAN LIFE FORMS POPULATING THE BIBLE

"Of course dolphins are more intelligent than humans. You'll never catch them opening up underwater theme parks where they teach humans to catch hamburgers in their mouths."
-- Swami Beyondananda

There's quite a lot to learn from the Bible when it comes to some of the non-human life forms that once lived or continue living here on planet earth. For example, God only knows how many species have disappeared from the face of the earth due to falling off the edges, especially those precariously close to the four corners (Rev. 7:1). These should no doubt have been far more careful. Too late now! But at least dragons and unicorns from the biblical days of yore are still around.

Whether creatures are seen as common or uncommon, the Bible amply demonstrates, as you'll see shortly, that treating them with kindness and respect is only for bleeding heart liberals -- you know, the so called "progressives." Animals and other creatures are, from biblical perspective, to be used, abused, and, whenever possible, deployed as weaponry against one's enemies. Even marvelous, magical beings like a certain

snake and a donkey, both well versed in fluent Hebrew, get no special treatment. So called "livestock," on the one hand, and Berlitz School mammalian prodigies, on the other, are all fair game for being reduced to the status of dead meat, whether literally or figuratively. God is no respecter of persons called animals.

Never mind propaganda inherent in Genesis 6:19 which says that all the earth's creatures entered Noah's Ark in pairs, one pair each to be exact. As it turns out, this only turns out to be true regarding unclean creatures, the clean creatures being allowed to enter in groups of fourteen (Genesis 7:2-3), thus ensuring success in voting out any lower cleanliness standard suggested, for example, by the deodorant-averse ferrets.

Ferrets are found on the list of unclean animals in the Bible (Leviticus 11:30). By becoming clean, the poor creatures might have been put on the menu so they wisely chose not to shower and this is why they smell the way they do.

The Ark was 450' long x 75' wide x 45' high, but only had one window (Genesis 6:16). The city building code department would have been all over Noah, if only their employees hadn't all been dead, as in drowned.

Noah at first seems to be something of a conservationist, preserving all the world's animal endangered species. Unfortunately, as soon as the Ark reaches dry land, Noah begins stupidly sacrificing a portion of the animals he had saved (Genesis 8:20).

There is a fiery serpent mentioned in Numbers 21:6. Whether or not this is a sibling of Pete's Dragon remains mysteriously unclear.

Teaching us the kind of science which we've been deplorably denied by the modern public education system, the Bible brilliantly warns us about a dangerous two-headed dragon with a rooster's head named a cockatrice (Isaiah 11:8, 14:29, 59:5). Alleged biblical truth aside, however, it can be argued from silence that the cockatrice didn't receive a lot of birthday invitations.

In Amos 9:30, we find Yahweh commanding shy serpents to come up from the bottom of the sea and inject people with deadly venom. Bad as this may sound, can you imagine how much worse things would have been had the serpents not been shy?

The Holy Bible seems to run dreadfully a-foul or "a-fowl" of scientific fact by confusing creatures like chickens (and even insects) with four legged creatures (Leviticus 11:20-23). Without a leg or legs to stand on, fundamentalists often claim that the biblical version of multifaceted reality is true simply because the Bible says it is.

In Numbers 22:28-30, we find a donkey who is highly skilled in conversation, aspiring to avoid further punishment or even death at the hands of the wicked prophet Balaam. The short verbal exchange between the two is far less pleasurable than the kind we'd later witness between the talking horse, Mr. Ed and his biped companion Wilbur.

When Jesus Christ so insensitively engineered the death of a herd of pigs by filling them with exorcised demons, these creatures must have been bewildered at finding themselves rushing headlong over an embankment to their drowning (Matthew 8:32 (RSV). Pigs, after all, had been banned from both Galilee and Judea, and were thus to be considered contraband.

Since the Bible frankly informs us that earth has four corners (Rev. 20:8) and is presumably flat (Job 28:24), we can assume that the world's unicorns (Deuteronomy 33:17) had the wherewithal not to slip and fall off the edges. He that hath an ear, let him hear.

In Genesis 1:30, the biblical God declares that he has given vegetarian food for all of earth's creatures to eat. The standing ovation from PETA and other animal rights organizations aside, the carnivores were likely mad as hell and plotted revenge.

Originally, all creatures on earth were given green herb as food (Genesis 9:3). This caused so much depression among carnivores, some likely wanted to die and go to the Islamic paradise where chicken is apparently served.

As punishment for tempting our prototype parents Adam and Eve into original sin, the serpent is cursed to eat dust (Genesis 3:14). Still, dust wasn't quite as bad as a lot of the cuisine one finds in haggis-friendly Scotland.

The biblical God would assure us that it's fine to snatch infant birds from their mother and presumably eat them, but we are to leave the mother bird alone (Deuteronomy 22:6). That way you can later take, kill, and eat her future young as well, praise the Lord.

In 2 Kings 2:23-25, the prophet Elisha magically deploys a compliant she-bear as his sharp-clawed tool in slaughtering forty-two children whose only crime had been to make fun of the prophet's hair loss. If the kids' parents had only brought the prophet a more generous supply of Rogaine a few months earlier, their disrespectful little brats might have been allowed to live!

You must not muzzle an ox to keep it from eating as it treads out the grain (Deuteronomy 25:4). On the other hand, if the castrato starts trash talking you, it's probably okay to return the favor.

On the seventh day, the Sabbath, everyone including the donkey, ox, child of the servant girl, and even the alien, is to rest (Exodus 23:12). If, however, the alien is restlessly homesick for the Pleiades or Ursa Minor, this may be difficult.

It's clear from Isaiah 1:3 that the ox knows its owner and the donkey, it's master's crib. Why the master is still in a crib or even a playpen would be anyone's guess, and same with whether or not the ox and owner happen to be on a first name basis.

The Holy Bible tells us that Gideon rose up and set his sons and wives on camels (Genesis 31:17). Surprised by this uprising and having been rudely set upon, the camels likely rallied and fought back bravely.

Yahweh orders Joshua to (cruelly) hamstring his enemies' horses and burn their chariots with fire (Joshua 11:6 RSV). The divinely inspired cruelty to animals aside for a brief moment, there's little doubt that trying to burn the chariots with water would have been a bitch!

In Leviticus 16:21 we find the Israelites high priest laying hands on a goat, but not for purposes of holistic healing or because he couldn't find a date for Saturday night. Rather, it was done as part of a scapegoat ritual in which the tribe transferred all its sins onto the poor creature, which was then booted out of camp.

Isaiah 11:6-7 tells us that in the coming day, the wolf and the lamb will co-habit, the leopard will lie down with the baby goat, and both the calf and the yearling will be safe with the (unsupervised) child. Speaking somewhat less optimistically as he misquotes Isaiah, Woody Allen says that the lion may lie down with the lamb, but the lamb won't likely be getting much sleep.

In Leviticus 11:13-19 we find a bat being referred to as a bird. Although modern science argues that this claim is a bit batty and is for the proverbial birds, people of unbending biblical faith often disagree, even vehemently so.

Forget about Lions and Tigers and Bears. Far from Oz, in the vision of Daniel's apocalypse, we find a more menacing lion, bear, leopard, and fourth creature -- an ugly one with ten horns and a really bad attitude (Daniel 7:20).

Jesus Christ frankly asks, "Are you straining (out) a gnat but swallowing a camel?" (Matthew 23:24) Maybe try vegetarianism inasmuch it's much easier on the digestive tract.

On one ghastly occasion for sick sacrificial celebration, King Solomon put under the kingdom's deadly knife, and without anesthesia, no less than 22000 cattle and 120000 sheep and goats

(1 Kings 8:63). No one need ever accuse Solomon of being a wimpy animal rights' activist.

According to James 3:7, all kinds of animals, birds and reptiles have apparently been tamed by mankind. This is especially true regarding the cassowaries, saltwater crocodile, and Komodo dragon, the majority of these now serving as social workers and philanthropists.

The biblical God has given you permission to snack on any kind of locust, grasshopper and cricket (Leviticus 11:22) save of course Jiminy Cricket. But you might want to brush your teeth before kissing anyone.

The biblical God is sending those serpents and cockatrices too clever to be charmed, to cordially bite you (Jeremiah 8:17). The silver lining is, since cockatrices are mythological, your problem is largely half solved.

Chaper Fourteen: REVELATION: THE LAST FRIGGIN' BOOK OF THE BIBLE, THANK GOD

"So the Rapture didn't happen. Cheer up. It's not the end of the world."
--Swami Beyondananda

The book of Revelation (The Apocalypse of John) was written at a time the early Christians were being harassed by the Roman Empire and likely feeling both hurt and angry, the magic of forgiveness often having its limits under pressure. Revelation is by far the most deeply disturbing, hostile book in the Bible on account of its willingness to inflict, not just grotesque reports of physical violence on the reader, but also soul death or, more accurately, the living-death of eternal punishment in a projected psychotic hell. Are we having fun yet?

Any false optimism aside, Revelation presents us with an unmistakably morbid view of the world, or, more precisely, the end of the world. It gives the reader quite a lot of poisonous eschatological material to chew on and to swallow at his or her own risk. If you take the writer's claim seriously, the net result can be ending up in an ontological straight jacket, far more concerned about personal salvation than is healthy for a good soul aspiring to live in the absence of Skinnerian Behaviorism shamefully presented as religion.

Revelation is essentially the conflation of two types of apocalyptic writings. The first type is characterized by giving the reader a panoramic view of heaven, one designed to sell the notion that the events here on earth have been predetermined from above. The second type generally features scenarios in which a so-called prophet is shown the alleged future course of history right up to the alleged end.

Inasmuch as I hate to break the news to Christians not-in-the-know, apocalyptic thrillers like Revelation have been pretty much commonplace in the Judeo-Christian tradition. The big whoop-de-doo about Revelation almost certainly stems from the fact that it is the only writing of its kind in the Bible, the other 'dime-a-dozen' apocalypses not having been included. In the big eschatological picture, Revelation is hardly unique, the same being true about its warning to take its teachings dead seriously upon flaming penalty of eternal damnation. While attacking Satan and his angels, Revelation actually delivers the reader into the hellish realm of destiny-driven belief, one in which there is definitely no bandwidth or intent to move mountains of bullshit through good old-fashioned faith.

The assorted, sordid issues raised by reading Revelation are too numerous to list, but here are the biggies: 1) It endorses the vision of global theocracy, even a brutality-friendly version of religious Stalinism; 2) It endorses mass extermination of humans and other creatures -- some of the violence targeting the biblical God's intended victims, but other being indiscriminate; 3) It presents as both desirable and inevitable the biblical God and His hit angels' future conducting of the most massive campaign of environmental terrorism since the Great Flood; 4) It reinforces belief in the kind of dualistic world view that pretty much assures perpetual conflict and destruction as the brick and mortar of self-fulfilling prophecy.

To add profound insult to horrific injury, Revelation isn't even well written, although it would still be something of a miracle if the Apostle John, an illiterate Aramaic-speaking peasant (Acts 4:13), really did write it, and in Greek nonetheless! Perhaps John went the Berlitz route in learning to speak it first. In any case, lampooning Revelation and its cast of characters seems like a good thing to do to help jumpstart a comedy ending to the Armageddon Script, the kind which breaks salvation-obsessed Christianity's hypnotic spell on countless innocent souls who have been cursed to take this bizarre book seriously. But taking Revelation seriously should be much harder than it has seemed to be for souls to do, given that the book is attention deficit-disordered in the extreme. As an example, please note that by Chapter 6, the sky has been folded up like a scroll. This ought to be puzzling to weathermen of the Christian faith, not least because there's still sixteen more chapters to go! Trying to make chronological sense of Revelation is senseless and I'll not even try.

Although there is nothing in Hebrew scripture suggesting that the Jewish Messiah would need to visit earth twice, having failed in His mission the first time, Jesus Christ seems in need of breaking the messianic mold. But unapologetic theocrat that Jesus is, He'll apparently be ruling with an iron rod second time around, shattering the nations like pieces of pottery (Revelation 2:27). Enjoy life while you can! Or better yet, smell the bullshit and conclude that the con job called Revelation is not quite your cup of tea.

In Revelation 12:3, we meet a red dragon with seven heads and by inference seven mouths to feed. This dragon causes consternation, not to speak of huge profit losses, for restaurant owners sporting all-you-can-eat salad bars.

Apparently being something of a talented artist, the dragon draws the third part of the stars of heaven with his tail (Revelation 12:4).

After his art exhibition, these stars are cast down to earth, which has to be a bitch!

In Revelation 7:1, we find four angels standing on the four corners of the flat earth. Since they have wings and thus can fly, they have no fear whatsoever of falling off any of the four edges except in cases where a few of them may have tied on one too many.

There's an angel from the east who instructs the four killer angels not to hurt the earth, sea or trees till the servants of their God had been protectively sealed in their foreheads (Revelation 7:3). The value of spiritual lamination aside, it seems a little late for this, not least because by this point a quarter of the earth and presumably a percentage of the Elect have already been destroyed.

With the sounding of one of the numerous trumpets blown in Revelation, namely, the sixth, the four killer angels are released on Yahweh's command from the river Euphrates (Revelation 9:14-15), although it's unclear why these angels were river bound in the first place. Suffice it to say, even if they can swim, it would no doubt take them an eternity to blow dry their own wings.

When the seventh angel sounds his trumpet (not flute or piccolo), there are great voices heard in heaven, but we're not talking karaoke or Star Search here. The voices are simply communicating that the kingdoms of this world have become the kingdoms of the biblical God and His Christ who will now reign forever (Revelation 11:15), democracy apparently being dead.

An angel comes down from heaven clothed in a cloud and wearing a rainbow for a hat (Revelation 10:1). The angel's face is of the sun and his feet are as pillars of fire, the later feature causing his podiatrist to prudently use fire retardant gloves when treating him.

The four angels are holding the wind so that it can't blow (Revelation 7:1), which, quite frankly, is no small feat. It quickly becomes clear to would-be green investors that wind power technology is simply for the birds.

One of the angels who sounds his trumpet causes one third of the sun to be smitten, and both the stars and moon to be darkened (Revelation 8:12). Another angel flies about saying what must have seemed obvious enough by now: "Woe, woe to the inhabitants of earth." (Revelation 8:13)

Seven trumpets (each representing seven judgments) are given to each of seven angels by the biblical God (Revelation 8:2). Before the drama is over, living entities having faith in the power of nonjudgment will almost certainly long to hear the occasional sound of a saxophone or trombone, but to no avail.

There are four horsemen in the book of Revelation and the one riding on a white horse is given a crown (Revelation 6:2). From his perspective, this was no doubt preferable to a root canal, the latter being a much more painful procedure.

The rider on the white horse goes forth conquering and in so doing sports a bow (Revelation 6:2). He's no doubt hoping he'll not run into enemies with high power ordnance or even AK-47s.

The guy riding on a bright red horse is given the power to incite folks to kill each other and otherwise take away peace from the earth (Revelation 6:4). But since killing has been commonplace here since time immemorial and peace therefore sparse, the rider doesn't need a helluva lot of skill.

There is also a rider on a black horse and he is holding a scale (Revelation 6:5), which means, at best, he is riding one handed. Oddly enough, there's no mention of him being pulled over by the police for reckless riding.

We meet a hellbent character named Death who is riding a pale horse (Revelation 6:8). Bad as this dude is, just think how much worse things would have been had his horse not been suffering from anemia.

Revelation warns sinners of the Second Death (Revelation 21:8). On the other hand, Hebrews 2:9 says that believers in Christ need not fear the Second Death, which is just as well since the first death gives them plenty to worry about already.

In Revelation 22:17, Jesus Christ tells the thirsty to come and accept the free gift of the Water of Life. Of course there's a penalty for not accepting this alleged free gift, and this being eternal damnation, it is to be considered substantially costlier than, for example, late enrollment in Part D, Medicare.

If your name is written in the Book of Life, you'll confusingly receive a new name and it will be written on a white stone (Revelation 2:17). The print job would no doubt have been a lot easier using paper, but stone will have to do.

In the vision of apocalyptic Christianity, whosoever's name is not written in the Book of Life is cast into the Lake of Fire (Revelation 20:15). But two unintended benefits innate to experiencing this fate are, you'll have instant access to toasting marshmallows and, more importantly, your heating bill will be significantly lower than it had been here on earth.

Death is given power over a fourth part of the earth to kill humans and other beasts with a sword and hunger and death. Killing people and other creatures with death proved the most direct course of action by far.

In Revelation, we find hybrid human-locusts riding around on horses showing up in mass, and these have the hair of women, the faces of men and the teeth of lions (Revelation 9:8). Specialty dental clinics which also offer hair salon services begin springing up everywhere.

Earth is attacked by myriads of these designer locusts which ride, perhaps uncomfortably, on war horses while wearing crowns of gold (Revelation 9:7). The ensuing terror and mayhem aside, it's a blessing for the precious metals market, which quickly skyrockets.

The locust people have a king whose abode is the Bottomless Pit, and this royal's name is Abaddon, which in the Greek is Apollyon

(Revelation 9:11). No mention is made as to whether or not the kingdom below is a constitutional monarchy or something more similar to Jesus Christ's aspiring theocratic realm of the iron rod.

The fact that there was at least one war in heaven (Revelation 22:17) means there could be more coming. And if this occurs, the homeowner's premium on your heavenly abode will likely skyrocket, not to mention your resale value dropping dramatically!

A star is given the key to the bottomless pit (Revelation 20:1). But being a star, it would logically have had no hands with which to take receipt.

If you believe that you'll likely end up in Outer Darkness, just be aware there will apparently be lots of weeping there as well as the pervasive gnashing of teeth (Matthew 22:13). If you're heading that way, do yourself a favor and bring both a sturdy night guard and plenty of Kleenex.

In the case of the Laodiceans, the Lord says that because these folks are neither hot nor cold in their spiritual diligence, He will spit them out (Revelation 3:16). Why exactly the Lord has churches in his mouth is anyone's guess, but digestion issues must of necessity remain of concern to the Body of Christ.

Apparently in a critical mood, the disincarnate Jesus Christ fault finds to varying degrees with all the seven noted churches including that of the aggressive Nicolaitans which He admittedly hates and is glad the Church at Ephesus also hates (Revelation 2:6). If only He had put in a good word for the Nickelodeons, Christianity might be more lighthearted today.

In Revelation 7:9, we find a countless multitude of people from all nations standing before the heavenly throne, calling out for the salvation of God and Jesus Christ, the Lamb. This may well have been confusing and embarrassing to both the First and Second persons of the Trinity, not least because they had probably considered themselves already saved.

There's a whole lot of folks in Revelation said to have come out of great tribulation, and their robes are washed in the blood of the Lamb (Revelation 7:14). Now, since blood is better known for staining rather than removing stains, the collective dry cleaning bill of these people has to be horrendous.

There is a creature, a lamb with seven eyes and seven horns (Revelation 5:6). He's not much to look at in terms of physical beauty, but is smart enough to avoid both E-Harmony.com and Match.com, or even the bar scene.

The creature communicates to John that he must speak prophecy before many people, nations, and tongues (Revelation 5:9). Apparently well versed enough in human anatomy, John undoubtedly is confident that, nations aside, wherever he finds people, he'll likely find tongues as well.

There's the miracle of the Lamb (Jesus Christ) looking as if He had been slain standing before the host (Revelation 5:6). Now, standing without support after you've been slain or have even felt like it, is certainly no small feat, regardless of who you are, so let's give it up for the Lamb, ladies and gentlemen!

There are Two Witnesses of the biblical God who have miraculous powers, one of these being that they can stop rain from falling (Revelation 11:6). They thus receive a standing ovation from the denizens of Seattle, WA. and Portland, OR., and especially Mawsynram, India, the wettest place on earth.

A pregnant woman eventually brings forth a man-child who is caught up to God and His throne (Revelation 12:5). There's no mention of the woman reporting her child as abducted.

The child caught up to God and His throne is likely winded. Since He is scheduled to rule earth with an iron rod (Revelation 12:5), let's pray He never catches His breath.

Revelation turns up a sea of glass like unto crystal (Revelation 4:6). It is no doubt stunning to look at, but a bitch to clean, even with an infinite, theoretical supply of Windex.

There are four beasts in the vicinity of the sea of glass, and these four have eyes both in front and behind. This gives a whole new meaning to the idiom: "Having eyes in the back of your head", but more to the point, the beasts no doubt remain rich targets for opportunistic opticians and ophthalmologists.

In Revelation Chapter 17, we meet the "the great whore," the one who fornicates with the kings of the earth. What makes her so great goes unmentioned, but curious, dirty minds can only imagine.

The so-called whore has seven heads and ten horns. This no doubt causes some of the kings to finally commit, however grudgingly, to date more normal-looking women going forward.

In Revelation 22:12 Jesus Christ declares, "Behold, I come quickly." So much for foreplay, Lord.

In the company of four boisterous beasts, the Lamb opens the first of seven seals (Revelation 6:1). It is the most cunning use of one's cloven hooves in the entire evolution of the species Ovus aries.

When the last of the seven seals is opened, there is silence in heaven for about half an hour (Revelation 8:1). Buddhist, Vedic and Sufi mystics are forced to admit that heaven is not transcendent to time, after all.

The Tree of Life bears twelve manner of fruits, which it monthly yields (Revelation 22:2). If fruit salad is your thing, then the Christian heaven is the place to be, but beware of poor food combining lest you end up with gas.

The payoff for obedience to the biblical God, at least according to Revelation 14:12 is, you'll be given a seal. This is great news, not least because a sea lion would cost a lot more to feed.

If you add to the words of Revelation, you'll be stricken with a plague, and if you subtract from the words, your name will be removed from the Book of Life (Revelation 20:15). Since neither option is particularly attractive, you can always try multiplying or dividing the words, not least because no penalty is mentioned.

CONCLUSION

Appearances aside, this book was not created to antagonize what I consider true Christianity. I wrote this book to help upset the Garden of Eden apple cart, so that a better fruit of the human spirit might finally come up for consideration. The process I've used here, as you've seen, is reverse cherry picking: finding many of the Bible's verses representing its worst claims, assertions, and mandates, and running with these while waving a red flag. Not that there aren't legions of other problematic verses in the Bible. There indeed are! In fact, there are so many, I'm suggesting that Christianity do itself a big favor and simply dispense with the Bible, taking whatever verses with it that are salvageable!

Whether successfully or not, I've done my best to communicate herein that, stubborn Christian apologetics aside, the Bible is something far less valuable than it's so fanatically advertised to be, having for centuries now been misidentified by hundreds of millions of the faithful as a "holy book" and the Word of God. On close examination, the Bible is not a good choice for being a book to guide humanity, nor is it to be confused be with anything sacred and sublime. Nor can one reasonably say with a straight face that since the Bible also has many positive verses in it, the net result is a wash. Based on its own exceedingly exaggerated claims of holiness, the Bible can't even begin to pretend to break even, the point being, good verses don't nullify the bad ones! Rather, it's more that bad verses poison the biblical well, there being no way to remove the poison.

Christianity at its best is so much better than the anachronistic, oversold Bible, and really doesn't even need this scripture going forward. In fact, defense of the Bible only serves to stunt the growth of this major world religion, as does the obsessive emphasis of Christian fundamentalism on "personal salvation." Using the metric of loving service, I can say with confidence that one of the most "Christian" people I know is in fact located in consciousness somewhere on or near the boundary between atheism and agnosticism. His motive for being helpful in the world is not about purchasing real estate interests in a hereafter. It's simply to be of service to people in the here and now!

But think about it: isn't someone who gives freely to others in the absence of belief in a reward/punishment-oriented God actually coming from a cleaner "spiritual" place than one who, being in league with the priestcraft and its doctrine of religious self-interest, expects post-dated, otherworldly rewards for his or her investment? If one's primary motivation is to give in order to get, does it really matter what the medium for barter is? Whether one is investing in stocks real estate, bonds, on the one hand, or Jesus Christ's alleged treasures in heaven (Matthew 6:19), on the other, personal gain is the actual point, however skillfully it may be disguised as religious piety.

Perhaps, in growing up in a Christian household as I myself did, you were duly indoctrinated into biblical dogma, even before you were knee high to a grasshopper or Revelation-friendly locust, a gold-armored one on horseback. And maybe, in conscientiously aspiring to be a "good Christian" you routinely chose to tune out all the Bible's various goofy or, worse, shockingly unethical material the type we've traveled through here. You may have just glossed over the really tough passages in this scripture in a different way, trusting in the belief that, grotesque examples of scriptural offerings aside, "God will explain everything to you later". Or maybe you have found fit to dismiss all the bad stuff in the Bible as anachronistic and therefore irrelevant. It could also be that you simply allowed one or more of Christianity's legion ministries to (cherry) pick more of the "pleasant" biblical verses for you, presumptively those verses sugar coating this book's troubled reality.

Like all major religions, and even some relatively minor ones, 21st century Christianity remains big business, in fact, huge business! There are fortunes to be made by those most capable of deploying clever religious marketing techniques or simply riding on their own personal charisma, using the Bible as a mere prop. As the world of profit turns, sacred cows are not just the dubious property of the east; they are also very much alive and well in the west, north, south, and center, including the empty core center of so much "New Age" psychobabble. And let's face it: many of us have lived our lives entrained into brain patterns of belief in this, that, or the other brand of dogma. Virtually hypnotized, we continually allowed ourselves to be milked and bilked by religious marketers committed to convincing us, or keeping us convinced, of the most unlikely things!

I'm not trying to be harsh here. I have already admitted to you my status earlier in life as a salvation hunter. In that conundrum, I unwittingly flailed about, looking for someone or something that could assure me that the mysteries of life and death had been solved by those superior to me. In my quest, I became the near-perfect chump for this and that exalted teacher or guru, and their absolutism. Of course, as Dr. Martin Luther King once said, "Nothing is more dangerous than sincere ignorance and conscientious stupidity." At the end of the day, the true believer remains truly problematic. The German philosopher Friedrich Nietzsche saw this and implored us to have the courage to attack our own convictions. Roman emperor/philosopher Marcus Aurelius also saw this and said quite impressively: "If a man can show me that I abide in ignorance, gladly will I change for I don't desire to abide in ignorance."

Make no mistake, when you are inside an experience in the sense of having crystalized or hardened in your insistence that what you believe is entirely true, danger really does ensue. Such belief makes you vulnerable to manipulation by "saviors," "messiahs," "avatars" and also unscrupulous politicians needing to nest in a gullible base. As an example, while living as a Vedic Brahman in my twenties, I held a mighty odd view of creation, one much odder, for example, than the Big Bang. Based upon the testimony of Hinduism's earliest scripture, the Rigveda, I was convinced that Creation began with the existence of a gigantic male Being named Purusha. This deity is said to have a thousand heads, eyes, and feet. Imagine! And no, it never occurred to me at the time how much Purusha would ultimately have had to pay in optometry and podiatry bills, or even trips to the barber.

Of course there are all sorts of other creation myths, each claiming to be THE correct one. Let's sample just a few others here. The Bushongo tribe of the Congo River posits a God named Bumbo who apparently suffers from poor digestion or excessive drinking; the world begins when He vomits out the sun, moon, and stars, as well as plants, people, and non-human animals. And in ancient Egypt's Hymn to Atum, a very limber, flexible (Yoga-proficient) God masturbates into His own mouth, then spits out the semen, and voila; cometh or cum-eth the rain, you, me, and the rest. And in a certain Chinese myth, heaven and earth are hanging out together in an egg-shaped cloud; from the center of the cloud emerges a giant named Pan Gu, and thus emerges Creation, right along with tremendous Omelet potential for discerning chefs. There's also the Norse tale of Creation. In this offering, a giant named Ymir is slain by chief deity Odin and his brothers; being ecologically conscious, the group recycles Ymir's remains and out of these emerges the cosmos.

Do these various myths sound goofy beyond a lint-sized speck of credibility? No doubt! We all know these myths are ridiculous because, after all, the inerrant Word of God, the Holy Bible tells us that the truth of the matter is, a geriatric deity with a white beard named Yahweh (the one true God) brought Creation forth in six days, and in the words of Ernest Becker Foundation luminary, Dr. Sheldon Solomon, "took a well-deserved rest on the seventh"!

As the world turns, Sigmund Freud's closest collaborator, Otto Rank boldly extolled our species as, in essence, a theological creation, and he took quite a lot of flak for this! Far from hating religion, as, for example Freud did, Rank envisioned for us, not religion's destruction, but rather a less neurotic, more deeply moral, more fully human manifestation. He in fact suggested that bringing our neurologically hardwired religiosity to fruition will be foundational to any truly desirable change. In this regard, how much sense does it make to continue underestimating how much pain, suffering and destruction immature scriptures like the Bible are still causing in the world today, not least under the influence of political snake oil salesmen?

I so very much agree with Rank: we are indeed a religious species by nature, and this is the case, as Rank understood, irrespective of the existence of God or an afterlife. In the words of American poetess/philosopher Myrna Schlegel: "Yes... myth- the stories that capture the true we sense and share, and put into words that metaphorically get us there. But we want to make those words literal words and that's where we get into trouble... Don't mistake words that try to describe the sacred with the sacred itself. The sacred is beyond the page. Look beyond words to the sacred." Sure, we can continue trying to find the sacred in the wrong places, just as we can stubbornly insist on confusing tall tales with rich psycho-spiritual myths, but the sacred is at heart what we all yearn for, aware or unaware.

Time to clean up the mess we've all made of our religious myths? Jungian analyst/ author Robert Johnson has said that the best definition of a myth is something that is true on the inside without being true on the outside. If religion now goes the extra mile in relocating its myths, tucking them inside, and becomes humbler and much less aggressive in the process, humanity will be the better for it, just as it will be better off with fewer ancient scriptures that reek of decay. We each have to start somewhere in our reevaluation of the world. The fifteen-year project that has resulted in the book you've just read is my reevaluation, and I sincerely hope it has been helpful to you.

ABOUT THE AUTHOR

Paul Schmidt studied English and philosophy at Adelphi University in Garden City, New York in the late 60's and early 70's before spending over a decade in various religious sects including tenure as a Vedic monk in a Bhakti Yoga sect and as a minister in a counter cultural church that taught the reconciliation of all opposites. As a persistent seeker of answers to the question of how to transcend the mundane (or what he refers to as Mundania), Paul traveled extensively in the earlier part of his life, spending significant time in all of the lower 48 states of the USA, as well as in Puerto Rico. And he lived for a while in India. Paul spent almost 6 years as a celibate, with commitment to abstinence from all drugs and alcohol, and at another time extensively experimented with mind altering, mind expanding substances. As a person interested in the subject of death and dying, he has served in several hospice organizations and is currently a member of F.E.N. (the Final Exit Network). Other interests of Paul's include writing aphorisms and also, of course, shedding bright new light on the Bible and its influence on culture and society.

Made in the USA
Las Vegas, NV
17 May 2021